Family Constellations & Healing Generational Trauma

Real Life Stories & Steps to End Inherited & Ancestral Cycles

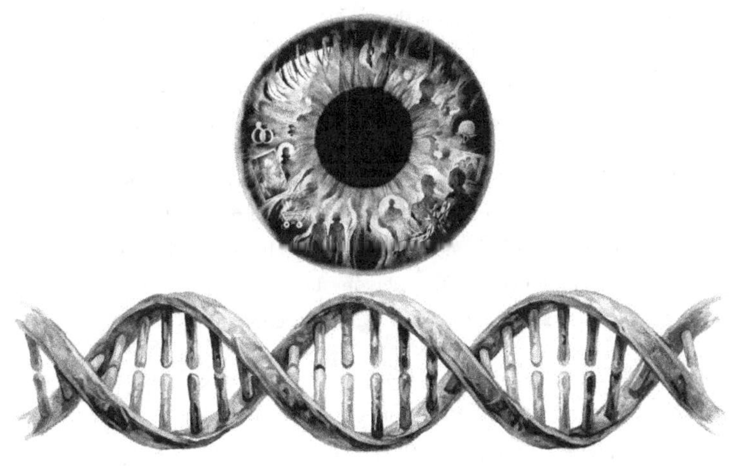

Ameet Aggarwal, ND

A portion of the proceeds from my books support orphan children and children living with disabilities and HIV, while also funding environmental tree-planting initiatives. To support these projects, please consider gifting a copy to your network, requesting your libraries and bookstores to carry this title, and leaving a helpful review online. Thank you.

Disclaimers

Professional & Medical Notice: The content of this book is for educational and illustrative purposes only. It does not constitute medical advice, clinical diagnosis, or mental health treatment. Always seek the counsel of a qualified physician or licensed professional regarding any physical or psychological condition. Never disregard professional medical advice or delay in seeking it because of something you have read in this book. Reliance on this information is solely at your own risk. The mention of specific homeopathic protocols or systemic interventions is for informational purposes and should only be used under the supervision of a qualified practitioner.

Content Warning This work contains detailed case studies and discussions regarding sensitive topics, including physical and sexual abuse, violence, murder and abortion. These accounts may be distressing for some readers. Please prioritize your well-being and proceed with caution if you have a personal history of trauma or sensitivity to these subjects.

Privacy & Identification: The stories in this book are based on actual client cases shared with express permission. To protect the privacy and confidentiality of those involved, all names, specific locations, and distinctive identifying characteristics have been changed or anonymized. Any resemblance to actual persons, living or dead, or to actual events beyond the scope of the shared case studies, is purely coincidental.

No Guarantee of Results: The outcomes described in these case studies represent individual experiences and are not a guarantee that others will achieve the same or similar results. Success depends on unique factors—including personal history and commitment—precluding any promise of a specific outcome.

ISBN: 979-8-9957892-0-8 (Paperback)

ISBN: 979-8-9957892-1-5 (eBook)

Acknowledgments

This work would not have been possible without the contribution and support of many individuals who have walked this path with me.

First and foremost, I wish to thank all my clients and students who so generously volunteered their stories for this work. Your vulnerability and trust have been the greatest teachers, and I am honored to share the wisdom born from your journeys.

My deepest gratitude goes to my late teacher, **Joanne Greenham**. Joanne taught me the art of Gestalt therapy; it was through her guidance that my awareness was refined and my intuition sharpened. Her legacy lives on and her Spirit guides me in this special work.

I also wish to thank my first Family Constellations teachers, Theo and Marianne, as well as all my other teachers. The foundations you provided opened my eyes to the profound hidden dynamics that shape our lives and gave me the tools to navigate them with grace. Beyond my immediate mentors, I offer my deepest reverence to Bert Hellinger, the founder of this method, and to the Zulu people of South Africa, whose deep indigenous wisdom and reverence for the ancestors are the very soil from which this healing practice grew.

Thank you as well to all the wonderful resorts and schools who have hosted my trainings and provided the sacred space necessary for people to receive this profound healing.

Finally, I want to acknowledge my family and my ancestors, for I stand on the shoulders of all those who came before me. I am deeply aware that I am who I am today because of their strength, their struggles, and their love; and it is within that same spirit of gratitude that I bow to my dear mother and father, thanking them for the deep love they share—a love that is the very reason I am here.

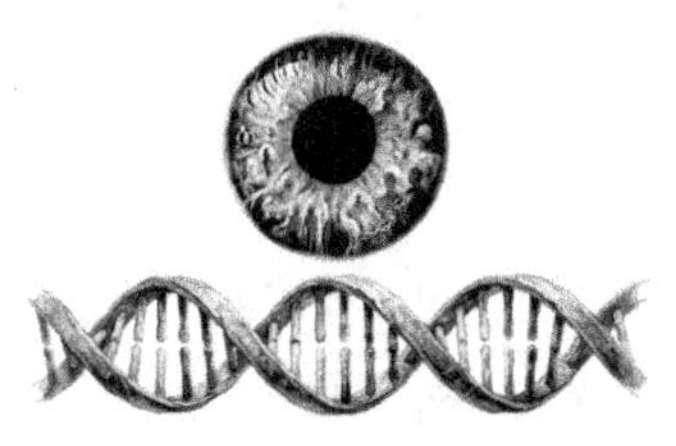

CONTENTS

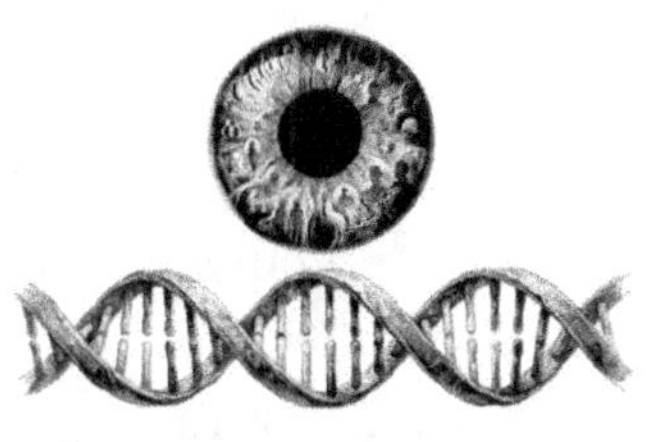

Preface

I dedicate this book to your Peace and Wellbeing...

This book is a warm invitation to step into your own liberation, offering you a path to freedom from emotions, health struggles, and relationship issues that cloud your life. It serves as a guide, drawing on over 20 years of experience in Gestalt therapy and intuitive healing, using real-life stories designed to help you *master the art of family constellations and the crafting of healing words that will bring about your deepest transformation.*

Inside, you will step onto the floor of the Family Constellation Session, watching in real-time as *the hidden roots* of chronic pain, anxiety, seizures, and even life-threatening illnesses begin to dissolve. You will enter **a sacred space where words become medicine** and where you will witness the exact breathtaking moment an ancient trauma releases and the flow of love heals.

Within these pages, you will receive a *step-by-step analysis of every constellation*, gaining a clear understanding of the *"how"* behind each entanglement and the precise intention behind the words chosen to bring about healing. This clarity provides you with the heartfelt skills to untangle your own life from the unspoken burdens of the past and reclaim your natural state of wellbeing.

Among the many transformative cases shared in this book, you will meet women like Violeta, whose overwhelming sense of responsibility and *chronic breast cancer* were a loyalty to four excluded siblings, forcing her to stand as the second child in the system.

You will witness Angelica, who, in a raw, somatic act of reconciliation, *curled up on the floor with her aborted child's representative* to release decades of guilt and reclaim *her right to be a mother.*

You will follow Inge, whose inability to fully commit to her own life was an unconscious *Blind Loyalty rooted in her grandfather's Holocaust survivor's guilt,* binding her to his fate of loss and sorrow.

You will meet Prisha, who finally *overcame her seizures* by reconnecting with the memory of the sister she lost in a car accident—moving from the heavy guilt of being unable to save her to a place of peace and honor.

You will also meet strong men like Daniel, whose childhood abuse was revealed to be a displaced symptom—a channel for the *unintegrated war rage* of his excluded great-grandfather. And Denise, who broke a toxic cycle of parentification by speaking a courageous systemic truth, finally claiming her true, light place in the family line.

Through their eyes and many other profound stories, you will see your own life, discovering that when the systemic burden is finally lifted, the body and spirit are at last free to seek their own way home to health.

If you are ready to put down the heavy burdens that *never belonged to you* - if you are ready to stop unconsciously living an inherited life - then turn the page. Your journey to your true place begins now.

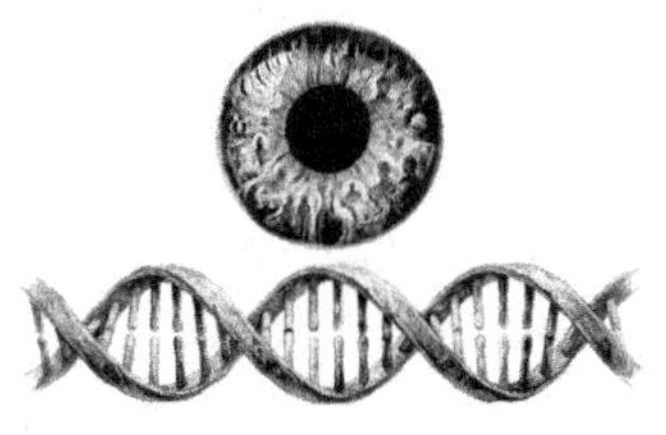

About Ameet Aggarwal, ND

Born in Nanyuki at the foothills of Mount Kenya, Ameet Aggarwal, ND, has spent over two decades refining a truly holistic approach to human wellness. A Canadian-qualified Naturopathic Doctor, Family Constellations, and Gestalt psychotherapist, he is recognized for his intuitive ability to uncover the hidden ancestral entanglements that contribute to chronic illness and emotional suffering.

He was recognized as one of the top 43 naturopathic doctors to follow because of his charitable mobile clinics for poor communities in Kenya and his approach to healing the mental and physical root causes of disease. By masterfully combining Naturopathic Medicine, Family Constellations, Gestalt Therapy, EMDR, Somatic Therapies, and Homeopathy, he facilitates a deep "soul-level" healing that addresses childhood wounds and transgenerational trauma alongside physiological health.

An international teacher and sought-after speaker, Ameet has been an invited guest speaker at various institutions, including Oxford University, and featured in numerous world health summits. He runs Family Constellations and trauma healing retreats and trainings around the world, while providing supervision for doctors and therapists globally.

He is the creator of the Mind Body Happiness Program, a comprehensive online curriculum in Family Constellations and Holistic Medicine for those seeking to restore physiological vitality and resolve the deepest layers of trauma.

You can stay in touch with him on his website www.drameet.com.

Why I Wrote This Book

Most of the issues that disrupt our lives—including anxiety, depression, chronic diseases, severe mental health challenges, struggles with relationships and intimacy, patterns of self-sabotage, and even persistent career and financial blocks—rarely originate solely in the mind or body of the person currently suffering. Instead, their root causes are often deeply embedded in **family or ancestral trauma**, an invisible inheritance carried within the family system.

I have dedicated my life to the practice of holistic healing for the mind, body and life issues, integrating modalities like family constellations therapy, naturopathic medicine, gestalt therapy, somatic therapies, homeopathy, and EMDR. After over 20 years of practice, I have been led to one profound conclusion: For long-lasting health and wellbeing, we must address the root cause, which is so often **our family trauma** woven into **our mentality, physiology and our deepest impulses**.

I have witnessed clients heal from cancer, chronic pain, relationship issues, infertility and even long-standing seizures once the systemic roots of their burdens were addressed. This has convinced me that unlocking and resolving these ancestral ties using Family Constellations is essential for a person's true and lasting healing.

The idea that we carry more than our own memories isn't just metaphysical; it's supported by science. *Epigenetics* now shows that the traumatic stress experienced by ancestors can literally alter the expression of genes passed down to us, predisposing us to mental and physical health challenges.

Furthermore, the discovery of *mirror neurons* reveals that we are neurologically wired to instinctively internalize and mirror the unexpressed tension, sorrow, or stress held by our closest caregivers. So when an ancestor or family member is injured, sad, traumatized, lost a child or a lover, or has gone through a difficult life experience, you, as a family member or a descendant, may likely pick up and carry this pain, grief, disease or even behaviour as your own. This is known as Blind Loyalty in family constellations therapy. And when there's Blind Loyalty in a family system, illnesses, mental health issues, life and relationship blocks begin to appear: they are symptoms of an inherited burden, forcing you to relive an ancestor's sorrow instead of living your own free life.

Similarly, when an excluded member—such as a miscarried or aborted child, an alcoholic, or a relative who committed suicide—is not honored or talked about, their powerful energetic blueprint remains in the family system. This unintegrated energy is then picked up by a later, loyal descendant and expresses itself as emotional or physical symptoms in their life, forcing the system to finally acknowledge the forgotten member.

The Universal Truth of Ancestral Healing

Even though the idea that the suffering of the dead can be carried by the living may seem far-fetched or "woo-woo," the concept of inherited, systemic imbalance is not new; it is recognized across many cultures around the world.

Within the **Judeo-Christian** tradition, this is recognized through the Hebrew concept of *'Avon*, which is often translated as "iniquity." In the Bible, it is described that the "iniquity of the fathers" is visited upon the children and the children's children unto the third and fourth generation. While often misunderstood as only being about moral "sin," the root of *'Avon* actually refers to a "distortion," "perversity," or "bending" of a path. It is a profound recognition that trauma, emotional weights, and destructive patterns act as a "bending" of the family line, passing down a systemic debt to future generations. In this tradition, the path to healing is found through acknowledgment and forgiveness—bringing these hidden distortions into the light to transform an ancestral burden into a blessing of grace.

Vedic astrology describes this systemic debt as **Pitra Dosh** (an inherited ancestral fault or debt), which is resolved through ritual practices like *Shraddha* and *Tarpan* (offering prayers and water) to ensure the ancestor's soul attains peace (*moksha*). In **Chinese Ancestor** Veneration, practices like the Qingming Festival and the burning of Joss Paper are performed to ensure the ancestors are honored and cared for in the afterlife, thus preventing misfortune and maintaining the familial flow of *Qi*. Similarly, in many **African Traditional Religions** (including the Zulu culture Hellinger studied), maintaining a harmonious relationship with the ancestors through practices like Libations and the Calling of Names is essential. This acknowledgment ensures the ancestors protect and facilitate the flow of their blessings and strength to the living descendants, ensuring the family line remains strong and vibrant.

These cultural parallels highlight a universal systemic truth: we must acknowledge hidden traumas and honor our entire ancestral system to reclaim our life force and be truly free—a wisdom now systematically validated through **Family Constellations Therapy**. Developed by **Bert Hellinger**, a Jesuit priest who studied the relational dynamics of the Zulu people, Family Constellations Therapy helps reveal your invisible ties and provides the tools to gently disentangle your own life from the traumas of the family system, while still maintaining a deep place of honor and respect for those who came before you.

Inside these pages, you'll witness the transformative power of Family Constellations through intensive, real-life case studies of profound healing. By weaving theory and deeper meaning directly into each story, I've made the complex principles of Family Constellations easy to grasp. As you journey through these narratives—covering everything from chronic illness to emotional paralysis—you will naturally embed this systemic knowledge, allowing you to freely embrace your own life.

The real-life stories captured within this book are drawn from the profound healing journeys of people who found resolution during my private sessions and intensive retreats held across the globe. Witnessing them heal layers of trauma and release lifelong burdens and diseases leaves me humbled by the power of Family Constellations. Every case is included with the full and explicit permission of the client, whose courage allows this vital work to be shared. **While some names have been changed to protect privacy, all identifying details have been carefully altered, and any resemblance to actual persons, living or deceased, is purely coincidental.**

I now invite you to step into this hidden world of healing the root cause by releasing family and ancestral trauma. If these stories resonate with a burden you carry, I encourage you to consider joining one of my life-changing healing retreats held globally, where you can personally step onto the floor and reclaim the life that is truly yours. You can also dive deeper into family constellations therapy, trauma healing and holistic medicine through my online courses. You can find all these details on my website **www.drameet.com**.

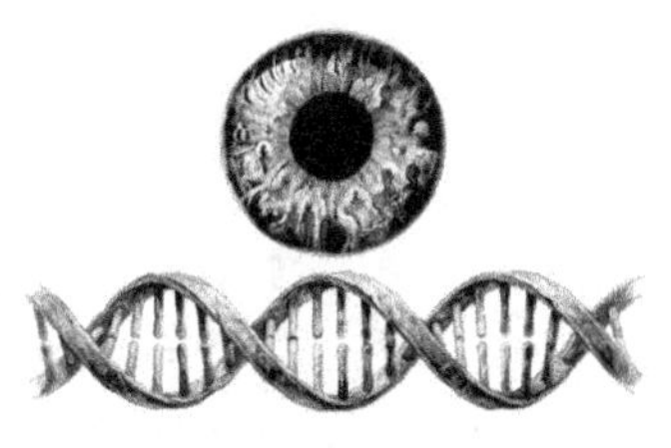

Chapter 1

The Orders of Love

To truly understand the healing journeys in this book and the process of Family Constellations Therapy, it is essential to first grasp the basic systemic principles that govern every family. These are not "rules" in the legal sense, but rather the natural flow of how love and life move through a lineage.

1. The Law of Belonging

This law tells us that every person in the family has an equal, undeniable right to a place in the system. This includes everyone: the living, the deceased, stillborn babies, aborted children, the "black sheep," and even those we might want to forget. When we exclude someone—usually out of shame, judgment, or the pain of a secret—a "hole" is left in the family soul. Because the family system seeks to be whole, a later descendant (often a child) will unconsciously try to fill that hole by "acting out" the fate of the forgotten person.

We see this dynamic unfold when a family feels deep shame about a grandfather who went to prison and they stop speaking of him; years later, his grandson may find himself struggling with unexplained rage or legal trouble. Without knowing why, the grandson is "remembering" the grandfather the family tried to forget. Similarly, when a miscarried child is never mentioned by the grieving parents, a later living sibling may feel a persistent, unexplained anxiety or sense of emotional incompleteness, unconsciously acting as the system's voice to remind the family of the excluded life.

2. The Law of Hierarchy and Order of Birth

This principle is about finding your "right place." It simply means that those who came into the family first have seniority over those who came later. Parents are the "big ones" who give, and children are the "small ones" who receive. Similarly, the first-born child holds a different energetic position than the second-born. When we stay in our correct place, we feel supported and "backed" by those who came before us. When we step into a place that isn't ours, we feel heavy, anxious, and out of sync.

We see this clearly when a daughter feels she must "parent" her own depressed mother; by becoming her mother's emotional caretaker, she has stepped above her parent. This reversal of order is why that daughter may feel constant burnout or find it impossible to start her own family—she is already "married" to her mother's needs. A different kind of displacement happens if a mother had a miscarriage or an abortion before her first living child was born, making that living child technically the second child. If the lost pregnancy is never mentioned or honored, and the living child is treated as the "first-born," this child may grow up feeling a strange sense of overwhelm, pressure, or "imposter syndrome," as if they are wearing a suit that is too big for them. Because they are unconsciously standing in the space of the first child, they lack the ease of their true position as the second. In this scenario, there's a profound overlap of the Law of Belonging and the Law of Hierarchy.

3. The Balance of Giving and Taking

This order governs all relationships between equals, such as partners, spouses, and friends. For a healthy bond to thrive, there must be a continuous, reciprocal balance of giving and taking. In the parent-child bond, however, the dynamic is unique because the child can never truly repay the gift of life; they only receive. Their healthy response is to receive that gift fully and pass that love forward into their own lives or to their own children. When children try to "give back" to their parents by carrying their burdens or emotional weight, it creates a reversal of flow that is both draining and unsustainable.

We see the consequences of this imbalance in a marriage where one partner is always the "helper" and the other is always the "needy" one. When the balance is broken in this way, the "giver" eventually feels depleted and superior, while the "receiver" carries a hidden weight of guilt. Often, the receiver may eventually leave the relationship simply to escape the unbearable pressure of the "debt" they can never repay.

4. Respecting Fate

Each of us carries a "fate"—the unique circumstances, tragedies, and joys that make up our journey. Respecting fate means looking at the difficult lives of our ancestors and saying, "I see what you carried, and I honor it as yours." When we try to "carry" the pain or misfortune of an ancestor out of blind loyalty, we aren't actually helping them; instead, we are turning away from the life that was given to us.

This often manifests in subtle ways, such as a man who unconsciously sabotages his own success because his father died young and broke. Out of a deep, hidden loyalty, his soul says, "I cannot have more than you did," as if staying small keeps him connected to his father's memory. Real healing happens when he realizes that his father's greatest wish would be for his son to flourish, and that he can best honor the family by choosing not to repeat the struggle.

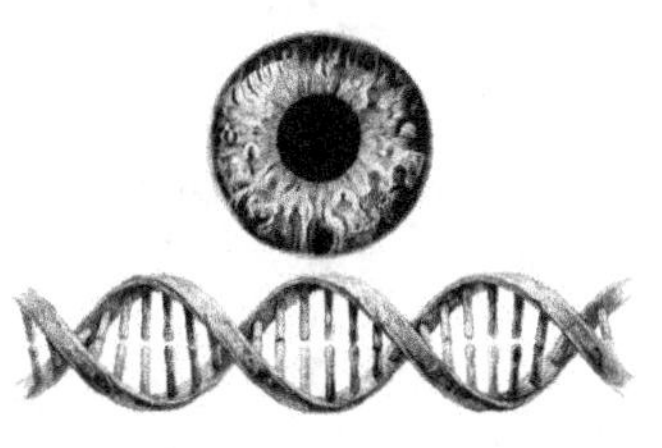

Chapter 2

Systemic Forces

Beyond the basic orders of love, there are powerful forces at work in the family soul. These forces often explain *why* we feel stuck, anxious, or burdened, even when our own immediate life seems fine.

Blind Loyalty

Blind Loyalty is the unconscious, primal love that whispers to a child's heart, *"I will not let you suffer alone."* It compels a descendant to carry the heaviness, pain, or tragic fate of an ancestor out of a pure—but misplaced—desire to belong. The motivation is beautiful, but the effect is devastating because it prevents the living person from finding their own happiness. We see this clearly when a person suffers from severe anxiety, not because of their own life circumstances, but because they are unconsciously carrying the frozen fear of an ancestor who was chronically anxious due to living through a war. They are feeling the feelings of the past.

Systemic Entanglement

When we are caught in Blind Loyalty, we become "entangled." This means we are no longer living our own life; instead, we are unknowingly re-playing an old movie script from our family history. The descendant reenacts the ancestor's unresolved experience without even realizing it. A profound example of this is a man who consistently sabotages his career success and health at the exact same age his grandfather passed away in a tragic accident. He isn't failing; he is unconsciously following his ancestor's timeline instead of his own.

Parentification

This is a heartbreaking reversal of the natural hierarchy, where a child feels they must "save" or support their parent. It typically happens because the parent is emotionally unavailable due to their own unhealed trauma, leading the child to step up out of love. It is a heavy burden for little shoulders. For instance, a child might become the family "peacemaker," the emotional confidante for a parent's marital problems, or the literal caretaker for younger siblings. This painful role reversal leads to deep burnout later in life and a lifelong belief that they must "work" to receive love/nurturing.

Competition

In the systemic context, competition is often much deeper and more desperate than simple sibling rivalry over toys. It is a maneuver to gain a parent's emotional attention when that parent is distracted by grief. If a parent is emotionally "frozen" or fixed on a deceased child or ancestor, the living child may unconsciously compete for the parent's gaze by identifying with that lost person's fate. Tragically, a child might develop a similar illness, manifest the same difficult behaviors, or develop an obsession with death, effectively saying to the parent: *"Look at my sorrow; I am taking on this fate so you will finally turn and look at me."*

Exclusion

Exclusion happens when a family member is pushed out of the family's memory or heart, often due to a tragic or difficult fate like an abortion, suicide, or a crime. The family tries to "protect" itself by forgetting, but the system never forgets. This act violates the Law of Belonging and creates an energetic "hole" that the system requires a later member to fill. For example, if a family attempts to exclude an ancestor who committed a crime or suffered from severe addiction due to shame, a later descendant might develop unexplained symptoms—such as self-sabotage, addiction, or an overwhelming sense of guilt. Without knowing why, this descendant is unconsciously attempting to re-integrate the fate of the excluded ancestor into the family's consciousness.

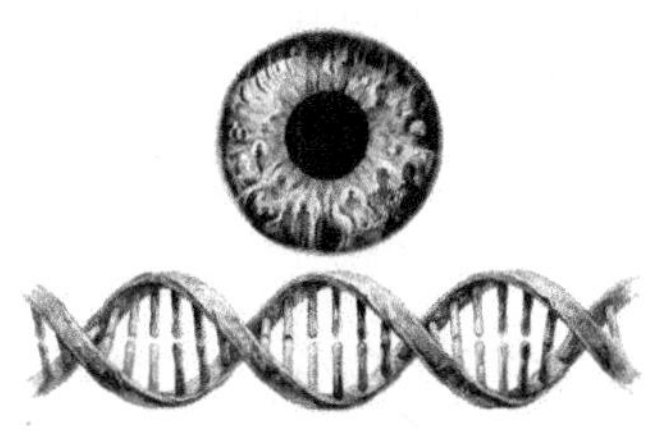

Chapter 3

Healing Sentences and Movements

These are the two primary tools we use in a Family Constellation to restore the systemic flow. Healing Sentences are precise, soul-level truths that the heart has been waiting to hear, while Healing Movements are the corresponding physical and energetic actions that support those words. These tools create a breakthrough in both the body and the emotions, restoring the flow of love immediately. In my practice, I usually channel these sentences and movements through intuition, and as you practice constellations more and more, you will also begin to sense them arising naturally within you.

Restoring Hierarchy and Releasing Burden

When a child has stepped out of their place to carry a parent's emotional weight, we use sentences like, **"Mom, you are the mother, and I am the daughter,"** to correct this reversal. This simple truth restores the correct flow of support—moving from parent to child—and frees the descendant from an unsustainable burden of responsibility. We see the power of this phrase with clients like Denise, who was caught in a toxic mother-daughter bond, or Violeta, whose burnout was tied to her overwhelming feeling of responsibility for her mother's happiness. When they finally occupy their "light" position as a child, the exhaustion begins to lift.

Addressing Inherited Burdens (Blind Loyalty)

To resolve the entanglement of Blind Loyalty, we must honor our ancestors without becoming lost in their pain. The statement, **"I see your pain, and I leave the burden with you,"** is used to acknowledge an ancestor's trauma or heavy fate with respect, while assertively returning the weight to its original carrier. This allows the descendant to step out of the past and claim their own destiny. We see this transformation in Inge, who speaks this sentence to finally let go of the immense Holocaust survivor's guilt that bound her so tightly to her grandfather's fate of sorrow.

Reclaiming Dignity from Perpetrator Shame

Sometimes, we unconsciously absorb the shame or responsibility belonging to a perpetrator within our family system. Sentences such as, **"I take my dignity back. The shame you carry is yours,"** are deployed to break this painful identification where a victim has unknowingly taken on the weight of a harmful act. This movement restores the client's innocence, asserts a clear personal boundary, and returns ownership of the act and its resulting shame to the rightful source. This is essential for a client whose great-grandfather committed a serious financial crime; by speaking these words, the client can release the inexplicable, heavy sense of personal failure they have been carrying and finally stop standing in for the family's excluded perpetrator.

Separating Destiny and Choosing Life

When a descendant is unconsciously bound to an ancestor's tragic fate, loss, or death, it can prevent them from fully committing to their own health and happiness—a direct violation of the principle of Respecting Fate. In these moments, the request, **"Please allow me to live my life fully,"** acts as a respectful but firm statement of separation. We see this in the ultimate statement of separation made by Inge; by speaking this to her deceased ancestors, she confirms her choice to live a full life, free from the shadow of her family's tragic losses. It is a way of asking for the ancestors' blessing to lead a destiny that is uniquely one's own.

Integrating the Excluded

The simple statements, **"I see you"** and **"I am sorry,"** are profoundly powerful in resolving violations of the Law of Belonging, especially regarding the exclusion of a deceased child, such as a miscarried or aborted sibling. While "I see you" restores the individual's rightful place in the family heart, the phrase "I am sorry" acknowledges the pain of their long absence and integrates that loss back into the family soul.

We see this raw, somatic moment of reconciliation with Angelica, who collapsed in tears while speaking to the representative of her aborted child. By finally looking at the child and saying, "I see you, and I am sorry," she moved through a deep moment of truth that allowed her to release decades of debilitating guilt. This act of recognition allowed her to reclaim her own right to be a mother and enabled the entire family system to fully embrace all its members once again.

Healing Movements & Their Effect

Just as words can shift the heart, intentional physical movements can shift the body's deep-seated energetic patterns. These movements are powerful because they give the soul a physical way to "act out" a new, healthier reality.

Bowing

A descendant bowing down to an ancestor, such as a child to a parent, is a profound physical movement that restores the Law of Hierarchy. This simple yet humble action signals a deep acceptance of the ancestor's seniority and the gift of life they passed down. By bowing, we unconditionally accept life exactly as it came to us, without trying to change or fix those who came before.

Stepping Back

When we find ourselves caught in an entanglement, the physical act of stepping back from a representative symbolizes a vital energetic separation. It is a bodily "no" to carrying what doesn't belong to us. This movement represents the conscious decision to stop carrying an ancestor's heavy burden, allowing us to see them with love while finally stepping into our own clear space.

Taking Your True Position

Stepping into your true, correct place in the Order of Birth is a movement that solidifies a new systemic reality in your nervous system. We see the immediate relief of this when a client who always believed they were the "firstborn"—carrying a heavy, senior weight of responsibility for the whole family—discovers they actually had three siblings miscarried or aborted before them. By physically stepping back from that oppressive "first" position and embracing their true, lighter rank as the "fourth child," they can instantly shed the weight of that misplaced role and feel the freedom that comes with standing in their correct place.

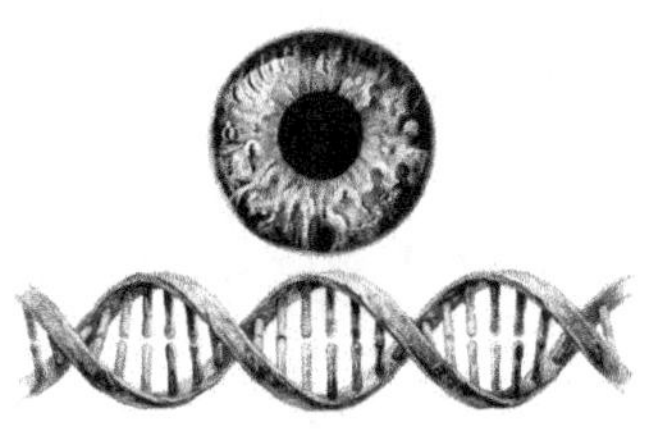

Chapter 4

Group & Individual Sessions

A Family Constellations session is a profound and transformative space where we reveal and resolve the hidden strings that bind us to our ancestors' unresolved pain. Whether we work in a group setting or in the quiet of a private room, the goal is the same: to untie the knots of the past so you can move forward with a light heart.

Group Constellations

The traditional method involves a group of people and relies on a beautiful, mysterious phenomenon known as the "Field of Knowing". This field allows the hidden truth of your family to become visible through the bodies and emotions of others.

We begin by briefly discussing your current struggle and your family history. It is important to look at the "heavy" events that impact the soul, such as lost pregnancies, early deaths, secrets, or even the previous serious lovers of your parents. I then invite you to select people from the group to serve as Representatives for key members of your system. You might choose someone to stand for your

"Mother" or "Father," but we also represent the invisible challenges you carry—such as an "Illness," "Chronic Pain," or even an "Issue with Success". You then gently guide these representatives by the shoulders and place them in the room based on your inner sense of where they belong.

Once positioned, the "Field of Knowing" comes alive. The representatives often begin to feel physical sensations or emotions that are not their own, but belong to the family members they are representing. For example, a person representing a "Grandfather who died in the war" might suddenly feel a deep cold in their chest or an urge to look away from the group. By observing these movements, we identify the Systemic Forces at play.

We then introduce *Healing Sentences and Movements* to restore balance to the system. These are not scripts to be memorized, but "key-phrases" that unlock the stagnant energy in the field. For instance, if we discover you have been carrying your mother's grief, I might ask you to look at her representative and say, *"I see your pain, but I am only the child. I leave this with you"*.

As these words are spoken, we watch for *Healing Movements*—the body's way of saying "Yes" to the truth. You might see a representative's shoulders drop, or they may feel a sudden urge to breathe deeply for the first time in the session. Sometimes, a representative who was previously "frozen" or looking away will finally be able to make eye contact with the person they were excluding, signaling that the Law of Belonging has been restored.

The session concludes when you, the client, feel a visceral sense of peace and lightness. This is your physical and emotional confirmation that the systemic knot has been successfully untied. You might feel a weight lift from your chest, a warmth in your hands, or a sense of "coming home" to your own body. Once your true place in the family hierarchy is secured and the burdens are returned to their rightful owners, the life force can finally flow *to* you rather than being blocked *by* you.

Individual Private Constellations

Family Constellations are just as potent in a private, individual setting, even online, which many people find more secure for sensitive personal work. Instead of human representatives, we use "Anchors"—simple objects like pieces of paper, stones, or figurines—to mark the positions of your family members and challenges.

In this intimate space, each object is thoughtfully assigned a role, such as "Mother," "Career Block," or "Anxiety". The access to the Field of Knowing is beautifully flexible here: you might step onto the paper anchors to "feel" the energy of that position, or I may use my own intuitive sensing to share the emotions and physical sensations I perceive from each spot.

We can see the power of this method when working with a **physical symptom or illness.** In an individual session, we might place one anchor for you and another for the **"Illness"** or **"Symptom"** you are experiencing. As you stand on your anchor and look toward the symptom, you might find that your body doesn't feel fear, but rather a deep, heavy sadness. You might even feel a pull to move the "Illness" anchor closer to you, or find that your gaze is being drawn past the symptom toward a space behind it.

Through this intuitive sensing, we may discover that the illness is actually acting as a "placeholder" for an excluded or forgotten member of the family. This reveals that your struggle is a form of *"Blind Loyalty,"* where your soul is using the symptom to say,

"I am suffering like you so that you are no longer forgotten".

Your body is essentially trying to bring a "missing" person back into the family heart through your own physical pain.

To resolve this, we speak healing sentences directly to the anchors. First, looking past the illness to the forgotten ancestor, you might say:

"I see you now. I see what you carried, and I honor it as yours".

Then, to release the shared weight, you look directly at that ancestor and say:

"You have done your job of reminding me of your place in this family. Now, I leave the burden of your fate with you. It belongs to you alone, and I am too small to carry it for you".

As you speak these words, you may feel a profound physical shift—the tension in your body might dissolve, or the "heaviness" of the symptom might feel suddenly lighter. This private, focused method allows you to separate your destiny from theirs, holding a sacred space for your body to finally let go of a burden that was never its own to carry.

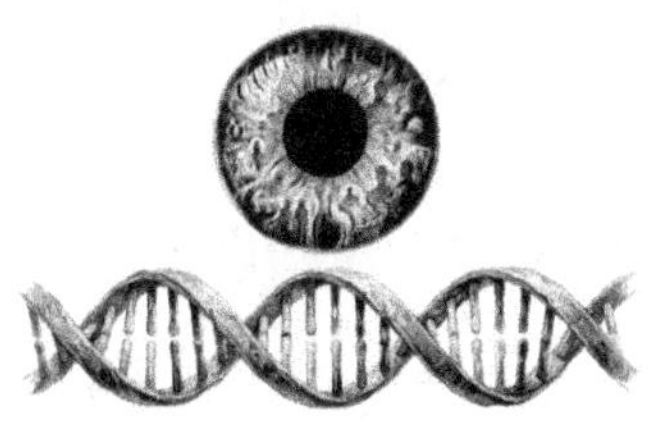

Chapter 5

Seizures: Prisha's Love For Her Dying Sister

The body, in its great wisdom, often speaks a truth our conscious minds can't bear to face. It was in this profound language that I met Prisha, a Soul deeply burdened by **right-sided seizures** that would appear as she was falling into sleep. These were not random events; they were a call to attention, a physical plea for an old, unresolved story to finally be heard.

Her History

Before even starting the session, I had intuitively felt that her situation had something to do with a sister. At the beginning of the session, after Prisha told me about her seizures, I asked her if she had any sisters or if there were any issues with her sisters.

Prisha was visibly surprised by the question. Her eyes welled up immediately, and she started to cry. This is the heartbreaking story she managed to tell me through her tears:

"It's true, I had a sister, but she died in a car accident when she was 12 years old. I was in the car with her."

I was struck by how her story instantly confirmed my intuition that an issue with her sister was central to her symptoms.

Out of curiosity, I asked: "Which side was she sitting on in the car accident?"

Prisha answered softly, tears streaming: **"On my right side…"**

We both knew we had touched on something profound. The connection was stark: Prisha's seizures manifested on her right side (the right arm and leg), the same side her sister had been sitting during the accident.

You see, from a trauma-informed perspective, the seizures were an interrupted, desperate, and loving attempt by the body to complete a defensive action that was impossible during the accident: reaching out to protect her sister, who was seated on her right side. Her nervous system, unable to process the overwhelming event, became a silent echo chamber—a physical yearning to save her sister. This beautiful, heartbreaking, and unconscious love story manifested as Prisha's seizures, a form of profound loyalty to that memory and a love that could never complete its protective gesture.

We both sat in silence acknowledging her profound unspoken love for her dear sister. I then slowly asked her when her seizures had started. She replied: *"When my daughter was twelve."*

We were both dumbstruck with this information – her seizures started when her daughter reached the age of twelve, the same age that her sister was when she died in the tragic car accident.

As she realized this, Prisha suddenly blurted out one of her deepest secrets: *"while I was pregnant with my daughter, I had a powerful dream in which my sister's soul seemed to be returning to me, to be reborn as my own child."*

It seemed that Prisha's Soul was treating her own daughter like her sister and was unconsciously expecting her daughter to die at twelve years old, the same age when her sister passed away.

A Path to Truth and Release

In our family constellations work, our task was not to fight the seizures, but to understand what they were saying. We approached the body's truth with great love and respect. The healing began with a gentle, conscious act of separation. I had Prisha say to her daughter:

"I am your mother and you are my daughter."

This simple statement began the process of allowing her daughter to be her own person, not a vessel for a departed Soul.

The next sentences were an act of profound compassion for herself and her past. The most crucial work was in her ability to forgive herself for what she believed she couldn't do. With deep feeling, I asked Prisha to say to her sister:

"I was too young to save you, and I give that burden back to you."

This was a sacred release of an impossible responsibility she had carried for so long. It allowed her to acknowledge that the event was outside of her control.

The most tender and transformative moment came with this sentence towards her sister:

"You're what's missing for me."

As she said these words, *deep sobs shook her entire body,* and a river of tears flowed, releasing the profound grief she had been holding for decades. This was the moment she gave herself permission to finally mourn, to acknowledge the immense void her sister's absence had created in her heart.

"That very night, after our session, I slept much better and the intensity of my seizures were down by about eighty percent!!", **is what Prisha told me in our next session!**

It was hard to believe, but her body, having finally been heard, was starting to calm and heal.

Homeopathic Support for the Soul's Healing

Later on, to support this profound inner healing, I used the homeopathic remedy **Opium.** In homeopathy, I match the patient's unique symptoms to a remedy that has a similar energetic pattern. While many different remedies could be considered for each isolated symptom, homeopathic **Opium** was the unique remedy that appeared across all three of Prisha's core symptoms, perfectly matching her entire experience. The three core symptoms I used to decide the most appropriate homeopathic remedy for Prisha were:

- Symptoms from the shock of seeing an accident: This perfectly described the initial trauma that began her suffering, and *homeopathic opium* is a key remedy for this type of shock.
- Ailments from the loss of a loved one: This resonated with the deep, unresolved grief she carried for her sister, and

homeopathic opium, amongst other remedies, is highly indicated for intense grief from loss of a loved one.

- *Trembling or twitching upon falling asleep:* This specific physical symptom, which perfectly mirrored her nocturnal seizures, is also a key symptom for the *homeopathic remedy opium.*

Homeopathic opium helped to support Prisha's emotional release from our family constellations session and helped to further transform the stuck energy from her shock and grief into more free-flowing and healthy energy till she was symptom free.

Prisha's story is a beautiful testament to the power of our inner world. When we can listen with compassion, and with the loving guidance of a soul-centered process like constellations and the precise support of homeopathy, the body can let go of its need to hold onto the past. Prisha is now free to live her life fully, to love her daughter without the weight of an old story, and to know that her sister's memory is honored not through illness, but through a life lived with peace.

To support deep emotional shifts like Prisha's, and Daphne's recovery from stomach cancer in another story, I sometimes include specific homeopathic remedies for shock and trauma alongside Family Constellations therapy. If you would like to learn more about combining holistic medicine with Family Constellations therapy to support your own healing journey, please watch my videos at **drameet.com**.

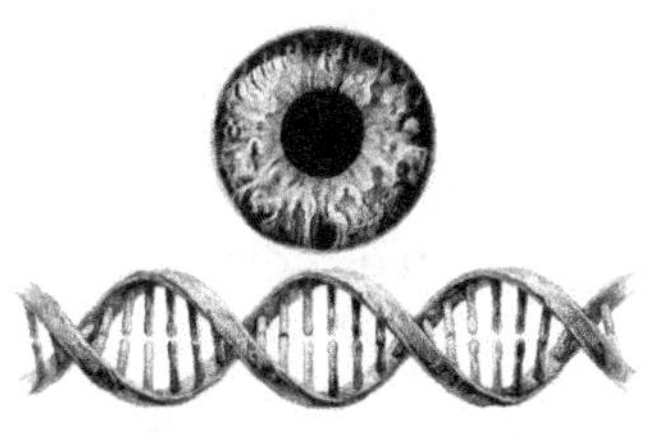

Chapter 6

Stomach Cancer: Indigestible Shock for Daphne

Daphne traveled to Kenya for a retreat, seeking relief from a diagnosis of stomach cancer. In the gentle wisdom of systemic work and German New Medicine (GNM), the stomach reflects our ability to "swallow" and process the world around us. Her body was speaking a truth her heart had found too painful to digest—an emotional shock that had become lodged in her very core.

The Hidden Burden: A Heart Divided

At the beginning of our session, I sat in meditation with Daphne. In that space of stillness, I intuitively picked up that there was a deep, unresolved issue with her father. Following this insight, I asked her directly what had happened between them.

It was then that the clear origin of the disease emerged: just a few months before the cancer symptoms first manifested, Daphne had discovered her father's infidelity against her mother. This revelation was a profound, "indigestible" shock—a massive emotional blow that her system simply could not process. From the perspective of GNM, this trauma was the direct biological trigger; unable to mentally or emotionally "stomach" the betrayal of the man she loved and respected, her body began a biological program in the stomach to manage the conflict.

The Dynamics of the Session: Speaking to the Soul

Because Daphne's parents were not physically present in Kenya, we worked through the method of *Systemic Representation.* In this sacred space, I stood before her to represent the energy and presence of either her mother or father, whenever she needed to speak to either of them.

The Path to Wholeness: Reconnecting the Flow

I guided Daphne through a series of healing sentences, coaching her to speak them directly to me as I held the space for her parents.

Step 1: Releasing the Mother's Burden Standing as the representative of her mother, I felt the weight of the bitterness Daphne had been trying to carry. I guided her to look at me (as her mother) and say to her mother:

> **"Dear mum, please bless me or look at me with love if I look at my father equally as a parent and take him back into my heart."**

As she sought this permission, the air in the room seemed to clear. I then led her to offer a tender reassurance and maintain her position as the child towards her mother:

> **"I am still your daughter and love you very much."**

She relaxed a little as the thought of guilt left her body.

Finally, I prompted her to acknowledge the truth of her own needs:

"I cannot exclude him anymore from me. Thank you."

As these words left her lips, a visible weight lifted from Daphne. She finally stepped out of the role of the adult mediator and back into her true place as a child. No longer torn between two sides, she was simply a daughter who belonged to both her parents.

Step 2: Accepting the Father Fully Next, I shifted to represent her father. Free from the weight of her mother's grief, Daphne could finally look into my eyes as the man through whom her life began. I guided her to name the trauma directly, asking her to say:

"I was surprised to find out what happened. It shocked me."

By speaking these words, Daphne began to let go of the sense of being blindsided. As she spoke, she stood up straighter, her spine lengthening with a quiet, newfound strength. It was a profound biological shift; her body was no longer collapsing under the weight of the secret, but was beginning to align itself for healing. I then led her to re-establish the bond:

I then led her to re-establish the bond with her father:

"I see that you are still my father."

To help her set down the load that had triggered her illness, I guided her to say:

"My mother's pain with you is not my burden to carry."

Finally, I asked her to acknowledge the high stakes of her rejection:

"It's costing me my life to reject you and what you did."

In that moment, a heavy silence filled the room as the gravity of those words settled into Daphne's consciousness. Her shoulders relaxed and tears rolled down her face as she faced a stark, internal crossroads: she realized that continuing to judge her father was a luxury her body could no longer afford. The choice was now hers—to remain anchored in a sickness fueled by resentment, or to grant her father a place in her heart for the sake of her own survival. She chose life, stepping out of the role of the judge to become, simply and powerfully, a daughter again.

The Miracle of a Restored Soul

The shift in Daphne's spirit was mirrored by a remarkable physical transformation. About eight months after our session, Daphne experienced an astonishing shift. Her tumor markers, which were significantly elevated, dropped drastically and she became symptom-free.

Her body, no longer required to "digest" a shock that wasn't hers to carry, turned its energy toward healing. While we supported her recovery with specific dietary changes and a single dose of the homeopathic remedy *Ignatia 200c* – chosen for its ability to overcome shock and grief – the true catalyst was the internal homecoming she courageously navigated within herself. By overcoming the shock of the marital affair and reintegrating her love for her father, Daphne allowed her life force to flow once again.

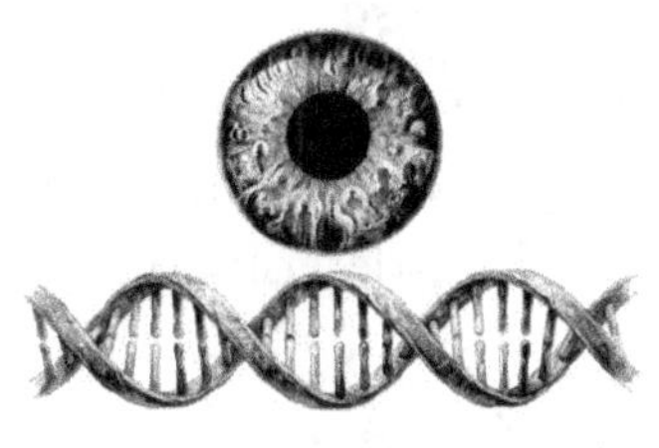

Chapter 7

Shoulder Pain: Sunita's Mother's Grief

Sunita was one of the loveliest and most genuine elderly ladies I've ever met.

Her left shoulder had been hurting for over thirty years, and she hadn't felt any long term relief with physiotherapy, homeopathy, acupuncture and other conventional treatments. There seemed to be no physical cause to her symptoms, so I thought we'd look at some possible emotional root causes.

Phase 1: Diagnosis of the Hidden Entanglement

Before starting her constellation, I meditated with Sunita for a brief moment. During the meditation, I had an intuitive image of her mother grieving a child. I then asked Sunita if there were any missing children in her family or if her mother had lost a child.

She was immediately surprised and shocked that this information came up.

"Yes!" she said, "my mother lost a child after I was born. I was one year old. The child was a boy."

Her confirmation made me suspect that Sunita was **unconsciously identifying with her mother's unresolved grief for her deceased brother**. Her chronic shoulder pain was likely a physical manifestation of the heavy burden of sadness she took on as a child.

Systemic Laterality Theory:

In Family Constellations, the location of a physical symptom often offers a clue to the origin of the entanglement. Pain or restriction on the *left side* of the body generally indicates an entanglement with the *mother's side* of the family or issues related to the *mother* herself. Conversely, symptoms on the *right side* often point toward the *father's side* or issues related to the *father.*

In Sunita's case, the pain was in her left shoulder, perfectly aligning with the possibility that she was carrying a burden of grief for her mother.

Phase 2: Differentiating Grief and Reclaiming Self

The important step here was to help Sunita separate *her own identity and sadness* from that of her *mother's overwhelming, primary grief.* This required Sunita to consciously acknowledge her mother's burden before establishing her own identity.

So I got Sunita to say the following sentences to become aware of the grief she was carrying for her mother and to connect with her own sadness for her unborn brother:

First, she acknowledged her mother's pain:

"My mother was very sad..."

Sunita swallowed hard. You could see she was somatically touching upon her mother's sadness. I then asked her to say:

"And I was sad too."

She took in a deep breath and let it out. You could see her begin to distinguish her own sadness from that of her mother's.

I encouraged her to feel her unconscious loyalty and the difference between their griefs by saying to her: **"Notice how you are borrowing some of her sadness"**. Sunita nodded her head in acknowledgement.

To help her further differentiate her feelings from her mother's, I got her to say to her mother:

"You suffered alone, Mum, and I joined you sometimes."

Sunita immediately remarked: *"This is not my pain! I feel my shoulder releasing a bit."* She was amazed at her own realization and the immediate change she felt in her shoulder.

The next step was to make her aware of how and why she was she was carrying the grief of her mother. So I got her to say to her mother:

"You cried a lot dear mum, for your dead child. I had to take it on out of love for you."

After she said this, she remarked in wonder: *"My arm is releasing a bit. My hand is not feeling so heavy anymore."*

This indicated we were on the right track, as the body was beginning to release the emotional weight.

Phase 3: Restoration of the Order of Place

The core blockage was Sunita's unconscious position as her Mother's *emotional caretaker or peer* in grief, which violated the **Order of Place or Hierarchy**. The final movement was to release this role and restore Sunita to the position of the innocent daughter, thereby empowering the Mother to carry her own destiny.

I knew we had to release her mother's grief and respect her mother's position as the older parent and authority. To help Sunita do this, I asked her to continue her conversation with her mother:

> **"You cried a lot dear mum, for your dead child. I had to take it on out of love for you…**
>
> **Not anymore, because you are brave enough to face this as the real mother of this child…**
>
> **I was never the mother to grieve like you did."** *(This sentence returns the heavy burden and the primary right of grief to the Mother).*

After saying these sentences, Sunita looks at me in surprise and says: *"I feel a release in my arm and shoulder. Half of the pain is gone!"*

I then challenged Sunita's old habit of carrying the burden, to reinforce the boundary. I said to her: *"You cannot steal the honor of being the mother of the child. It's her honor."*

Acknowledging this, Sunita reports: *"There's a tingling in my arm. Something is releasing."*

To achieve a complete systemic and emotional disentanglement, I asked her to say to her mother:

"Your grief and his death is no longer my responsibility. It never was."

Sunita's response: *"Feeling lighter."*

Finally, to help Sunita fully restore her position as *just the child and not the caretaker* of her mother, I asked her to *bow* to her mother and say:

"You are my real mother, so you can handle what is yours. This is a more real form of respect for your place in this family as the mother."

After saying this, Sunita said to me: *"A lot of the pain is gone. Tonnes of weight has lifted."*

By restoring the correct family *order of place* and disentangling from her Mother's grief, Sunita's pain was significantly less.

Phase 4: Integration and Conclusion

To help Sunita fully integrate her sense of position in her family, I asked her to tell me how many siblings they were, including the lost child. She said: *"After the unborn child, I had four sisters and then my youngest brother."*

To reinforce Sunita's sense of her entire family with the unborn child, I asked her to imagine herself as *one of seven children* and notice the feelings that came up inside of her. This act of including the forgotten sibling allowed the family system to become "whole."

She smiled: *"I already feel better saying that. I feel happy inside. I feel like smiling and laughing. I have a full breath inside of me."*

This illustrates the power of family constellations therapy: to release chronic pain that could be a result of emotions that are not ours to carry, and to strengthen our true sense of self by opening our hearts once again to those, especially unborn children, who have been forgotten.

This is Sunita's story. A lovely woman, entangled in her mother's grief since she was *only one year old* – a big responsibility for a little child.

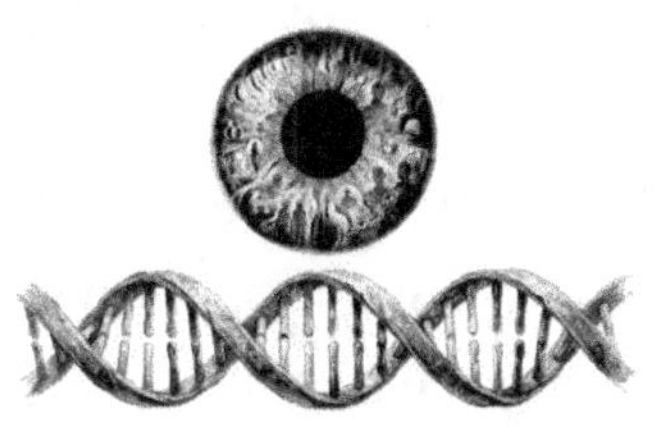

Chapter 8

Zombie Fatigue: Adela's Aborted Siblings

Adela, age 40, came to me suffering from a profound **lack of vitality and motivation**. Her main struggles included debilitating depression, pervasive procrastination, and a distinct feeling like a **zombie in the mornings** that took her hours to fully wake up. She felt a deep, persistent sense of low self-worth, as though she had no right to fully occupy her own life.

The critical insight from the Family Constellation work was the discovery that Adela's mother had experienced **two abortions** before Adela's birth. These two unborn siblings were **Excluded** from the conscious family picture, but they remained powerfully present in the Family Soul. The constellation clearly showed Adela was entangled with their fate.

Root of the Symptoms

Adela's suffering was a direct, unconscious expression of her loyalty to her lost siblings. In the Family Soul, the surviving child often takes on the fate of the excluded:

1. "Zombie" State and Following the Dead

The feeling of being a "zombie" and her pervasive depression are classic signatures of Following the Dead. Adela's soul was not fully present in her body; she was standing with one foot in life and one in the place of death, where her siblings rest. Her vitality and will to live were unconsciously drawn toward them in a tragic act of solidarity, leaving her depressed and unable to fully awaken.

2. Low Self-Worth and the Devaluation of Life

The deepest root of Adela's low self-worth lay in the message her system received about the aborted children. This feeling stems from two powerful systemic movements:

- **Devaluation of Predecessors:** If the lives of her predecessors were implicitly deemed not valuable enough to be allowed to live, Adela's own soul concluded: "If the lives before mine were not worth keeping, then my life cannot be of greater value." She subconsciously inherited the judgment of worthlessness placed upon the aborted children, which manifested as her inability to value herself or claim her space.
- **Tragic Loyalty: The Guilt of Betrayal:** Because her siblings were denied life, Adela's unconscious soul makes a tragic, loving vow: "If you cannot live, then I shall not live fully either." To thrive, to be happy, or to claim her full potential would feel, on a soul level, like a cruel betrayal of their short, unlived fate. This deep-seated inner conflict prevents her from truly feeling worthy of the great life she was given.

3. Procrastination and Survivor's Guilt

Adela's pervasive procrastination and lack of will are manifestations of Survivor's Guilt. This is not a logical guilt, but a deep, systemic feeling of "My life comes at the cost of another." By failing to realize her full potential or achieve success, Adela subconsciously minimizes her life and happiness, seeking to atone for surviving when her siblings did not. Any attempt at joy or progress feels like a betrayal of their fate.

The Sacred Fear of the Parents

The existence of aborted siblings often creates a systemic wound for the surviving child: a subtle, primal fear of the parents.

For a child, parents are the source of life, safety, and existence itself. When a surviving sibling recognizes that the parents terminated a family member, the child's deep conscience recognizes that the givers of life were also, in this context, the agents of death (or those who decided not to grant the right to belong). This shatters the fundamental security of the system, creating a profound, subtle fear: the source of life has become fundamentally unsafe.

This was also confirmed in Adela's constellation, where she felt a mistrust towards her mother and a tremendous amount of fear towards her father.

The Healing Movement

The healing path for Adela involved consciously acknowledging the true Order of Belonging and accepting her life as a gift. The therapeutic movements included:

Honoring the Siblings and Taking Her Place: The healing began with a sacred, physical movement: I had Adela lie down next to the representatives of her aborted siblings. As she lay down next to their stillness, her own Soul began to truly recognize their presence—a presence that is usually ignored in the family system. This profound recognition allowed her to finally fully grieve them.

As her Soul embraced this reality, I asked her to say:

"I see you, you belong, and I leave your fate with love."

Her whole body relaxed as she was able to return the burden of their fate to them without carrying it herself.

I then asked her to claim her rightful place as the third child, not the first, by declaring to her parents:

"Please accept me as the third of three children, and I can no longer live as the first child in this family. I take my place as the third child in the family."

This movement released her from the burden of the first two positions and allows her to live her life freely.

I also got her to say to her parents:

"These are all your children. They all had their own fate."

This final sentence gave Adela a deeper sense of peace, as she was no longer responsible for trying to "fix" the fate of her lost siblings and no longer had to try and "bring them back" to life.

Resolving the Fear: To help her resolve the fear towards her parents and to life in general, I asked her to say to her parents:

"I give the consequences of your choice back to you, and I take my life now. I am safe with you as my parents."

Something in Adela calmed. It was as if she had got herself out of a threatening situation or "reality" from her past.

To deepen Adela's healing, we could have also chosen the words *"I take the life you gave me fully. My life is my own, and I live it for myself. I am now free to choose happiness"*, which is a very powerful healing sentence to help a client disentangle themselves from an enmeshment with their parents.

The next morning, Adela reported feeling significantly less like a zombie when she woke up. When Adela returned for another retreat, she reported that her symptoms had improved since we had last worked together. As she continues to work on recognizing her true place in the family and honoring the fate of her aborted siblings, her symptoms will continue to heal. As she consciously gives herself permission to live and take in life, despite the fate of her siblings, her self-worth will likely grow, allowing her full life force to finally flow.

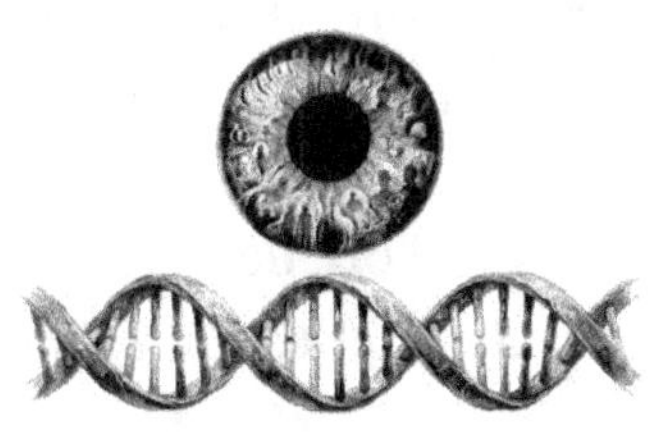

Chapter 9

Back Pain: Rumi's Love For Missing Children

The power of one individual's healing movement often opens a doorway for others. After witnessing Adela's constellation, Rumi was moved to address her own profound, unacknowledged loss: her two aborted children and one miscarried child. This therapeutic moment beautifully demonstrated the link between the family soul, the body, and chronic pain.

The Constellation

To honor the excluded children, I asked three representatives to lay down on the floor. Rumi stood there, watching them in silence. This initial silence was crucial, as it allowed her nervous system and Soul slowly to start to recognize the children as her own, breaking the common defense mechanism where people often fail to consciously acknowledge aborted and miscarried children as actual members of the family system.

Slowly, as Rumi's body began to register the reality of these children, she lay down next to them. Without any words, she slowly put her arm around them, moving into a deep, primal form of connection.

In that silence, she first focused on including and accepting each one of them into her heart. Only after this complete acceptance was she able to say a gentle, loving goodbye to them, allowing them to go to where Souls belong.

We were all silent as we watched this magical and tender moment of ultimate recognition.

After a while, Rumi slowly rose, a deep sense of gratitude and peace settling in her eyes. She had finally let them go, and in doing so, she also recognized her own value as a mother to three children.

As she stood, Rumi moved her shoulders around, her eyes widening in disbelief. She said: *"Gosh, the pain in my upper back has strangely gone. I've had it for over 30 years. It's like the burden has finally lifted. I had no idea it was related to this pain I was carrying on behalf of my children"*.

For 30 years, Rumi's body had held the heavy, rigid posture of a mother carrying the unlived lives and the unexpressed grief for her three lost children. The chronic upper back pain **was the physical manifestation of this unconscious burden carried out of tragic loyalty.** The moment Rumi's Soul recognized, accepted, and released their fate - by consciously returning the burden of their death to the *universal order,* restoring the *Order of Belonging* (by giving her three children their rightful, permanent place in the family system) and returning their destiny to the greater systemic field of life and death, where every fate is held and respected - the deep, muscular tension of three decades was released.

This immediate and profound physical release is a hallmark of successful Family Constellations work. In metaphysical medicine, the **upper back, especially the area between the shoulder blades, is the body's physical center for carrying burdens or responsibility.**

When a client is unconsciously entangled with the heavy fate of an **excluded** family member (such as an aborted child), they are essentially carrying the metaphysical weight of that trauma, that fate, and the systemic secret without realizing it.

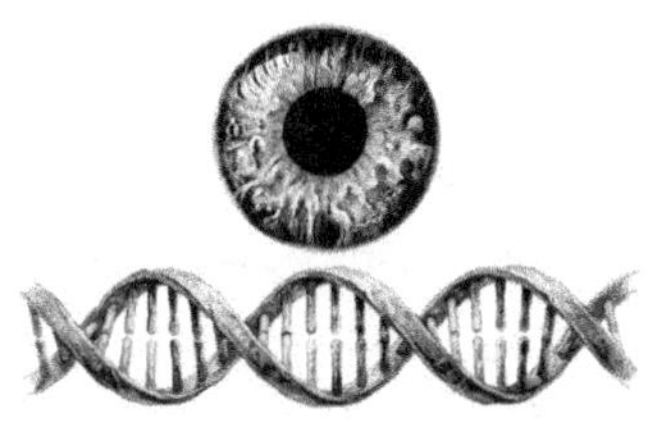

Chapter 10

Struggling To Live: Maisha's Birth

Maisha presented with a lifelong, pervasive feeling that she had to struggle to live and fight for her existence - a survival imperative that translated into chronic tension and an inability to truly relax or find ease in life. Her systemic challenge was a deep *Birth Trauma* involving an interrupted, forceful, and near-fatal arrival, leaving her entire system in a state of perpetual hyper-vigilance.

History and Context

Maisha's core trauma was anchored in the circumstances of her birth:

- **The Interrupted Birth:** When Maisha's mother went into labor, the hospital was overcrowded. The attending doctor instructed the mother to hold her legs together and physically stop the baby from coming out. This act, intended to delay birth, created an immediate, existential threat for Maisha, defining her first experience of the world as a place where she was blocked and had to fight to emerge.
- **Near-Death Experience:** When Maisha was finally born,

she was not breathing. The medical staff initially presumed she had not survived.

- **The Survival Imperative:** Because Maisha's first effort to take life was met with physical resistance, her body learned to associate birth and life itself with *force, fear, and a desperate need to fight.* Maisha's system registered this sequence (blocked, fought, died, revived) as her fundamental template for life: survival is conditional upon ceaseless struggle and battle. This survival state persisted into adulthood, making relaxation impossible.

Phase 1: Somatic-Systemic Re-patterning (The Re-birthing)

Maisha's constellation focused on somatic re-patterning of the birth event to complete the interrupted flow and rewrite her body's memory:

1. **The Block:** I asked Maisha to lay on the floor next to me as if in her mother's womb, and imagine herself slowly coming out of her mother's birth canal. I then held her extremely tightly around her arms, simulating the pressure of the birth canal and, critically, the *physical restraint* imposed by the mother. This allowed Maisha to somatically re-experience the feeling of being *trapped and unable to move.*

2. **The Release:** I then slowly eased the tension, allowing Maisha to use her own agency to push herself out of my arms, head first, mirroring a successful emergence from the birth canal.

3. **Completion:** Maisha finally crawled free, collapsing into the arms of the representative for her mother. For the first time, her system received the counter-message: *she could relax and breathe automatically,* without the feeling of fighting for her life.

Phase 2: Integrating the Body and Resolving the "Floating" State

The brief period of peace was followed by a subtle yet profound systemic symptom: Maisha said she felt like she was floating and not fully in her body. I felt that this was her system re-experiencing the near-death state in the hospital, the moment the doctors thought she was dead, suggesting a disconnection from life.

So, here's what I did:

1. **Re-establishing the Connection:** I asked the mother's representative to hold Maisha's lower back, while my hand rested on her belly, symbolizing the umbilical cord - the physical line of life that was not initially honored.

2. **Affirming Survival:** I asked Maisha to say the affirmation of her basic biological security: "I can still breathe through my umbilical cord." This brought an immediate shift, allowing her to relax a bit more and feel the weight of her body on the floor.

3. **Receiving Permission to Be Born and to Live:** I then got the mother's representative to deliver the ultimate healing sentence, counteracting the original block:
    "I'm ready for you to come – come when you are ready, my child."

    This statement was crucial because it offered Maisha's system unconditional permission to both arrive safely (to be born) and to accept her life fully (to live), replacing the initial message of "Stop!" with a foundation of welcoming and security.

Maisha began to sink into her body, the floating dissipated, and she breathed a deep sigh of relief. This completed the re-patterning. Maisha could then stand on her own, completely relaxed, having successfully replaced the survival template of "fight to live" with a new sense of unconditional security and uninterrupted flow of life.

Two years later, Maisha wrote to me with some heart warming news:

"Your session helped me immensely, and I have so much to be grateful for. I truly feel that since then I am living, not just surviving. I live without effort, everything flows, without major struggles or battles."

"Of course challenges always arise in life, but I feel I don't have to be constantly prepared to fight. I am living, being happy, and when challenges come, I deal with them, and I enjoy life when there are no challenges."

"I feel a greater "thirst for life," I want more for myself, I feel more abundant... I think I am truly living, and not waiting for the next fight. Thank you very much for everything!"

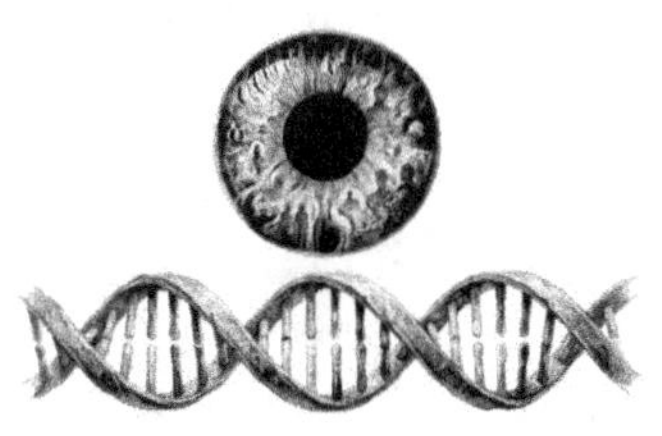

Chapter 11

Breast Cancer & Overwhelm: Violeta The Sixth Child

Violeta, a woman of deep sweetness, humility, and quiet power, came to several of my retreats. She arrived carrying the heavy weight of burnout and an overwhelming sense of responsibility, all while navigating the profound challenge of breast cancer.

She shared with me the burden she had carried since childhood: "I always felt responsible for the wellbeing of my mother, father, sister and everyone. I believe I'm the strong one, responsible, and I can bring my family together."

The air was heavy with grief as she spoke of her older sister, Elena, who had passed away recently. Her mother was totally devastated after losing Elena, and Violeta felt her mother's eyes no longer fell upon her. "All the love has gone away from the family now," she cried. Elena's own life had been marked by tragedy; she had endured a miscarriage, the loss of a daughter, and then, heartbreakingly, the death of her nineteen-year-old son in a car accident.

As we looked deeper into the family history, more layers of hidden loss emerged. Violeta told me: "After Elena was born, my mum had three abortions and one miscarriage, and then I was born. My mother is the third surviving child in her family, but before her, my Grandmother had a miscarriage."

Violeta's Systemic Issues:

To help you better understand the healing movements we explored, it is helpful to first look at the core systemic entanglements that were revealed within Violeta's family soul.

Although Violeta believed she was the second child, systemically, she is the sixth. She was born after four unacknowledged and excluded siblings. This misplacement is critical; the second position in a family carries a much greater systemic weight of responsibility than the sixth.

The core issues stemming from this history created a heavy "chain reaction" through the generations:

- **The Ancestral Wound (The Grandmother's Grief):** The pattern began with Violeta's grandmother, who suffered a miscarriage before Violeta's mother was born. Deeply grieving and entangled with her lost child, the grandmother was likely emotionally unavailable to Violeta's mother. This left the mother with a profound, unfulfilled hunger for maternal warmth—a "void" she carried into her own adulthood.
- **The Cycle Repeats (The Mother's Trauma):** Violeta's mother then experienced her own losses—three abortions and a miscarriage. Between her own grief and the inherited "emptiness" from her mother, she was unable to be fully

present for her living children. She was "looking at the dead," and as a result, her living children felt unseen.

- **The Law of Belonging & The Systemic Void:** Every child has an equal right to belong. By not acknowledging the four missing siblings, the family violated this Law of Belonging. This created a powerful energetic "hole" in the system that an alive child would unconsciously try to fill.

- **The Reversal of Roles (Parentification):** Because the mother's emotional needs were never met by her own parents, she unconsciously turned toward Violeta to fill that gap. This created a "Systemic Reversal": instead of the mother giving and the child receiving, Violeta became the emotional caretaker for her mother. It is an impossible, soul-crushing task to try and be the "mother" to the one who gave you life.

- **Blind Loyalty & The Burden of the "Strong One":** Out of a deep, unconscious "Blind Loyalty," Violeta stepped out of her correct place as the youngest (sixth) child and into the senior role of the "strong one." She took on the "Transference of Burden," attempting to unify the family and carry the weight of her parents' happiness. This misplaced responsibility is the ultimate source of her chronic burnout.

Illness as a Systemic Language

From a systemic perspective, Violeta's breast cancer can be seen as the physical manifestation of these deep, invisible loyalties. In family constellations, serious illness often signals that a child's soul is caught in one of two powerful dynamics:

1. **Following the Dead ("I follow you"):** When a loved one dies—especially a sibling like Elena—the surviving sibling may feel an unconscious guilt for being alive. Out of a "Blind Loyalty," the soul says, *"If you had to suffer or leave, I will suffer*

or leave too." Violeta's cancer was a way for her body to move toward the same "place" where Elena was. By becoming ill, she was unconsciously staying close to her sister, following her into the shadows of death.

2. **The Competition for Love ("Look at me, too")**: Because Violeta's mother was entirely consumed by her grief for Elena, she became the "most important" child in the family system. The mother's heart and eyes were fixed on the daughter she had lost, leaving Violeta feeling invisible.

In a child's desperate logic, being healthy and "strong" means you are ignored, while being sick or "dying" means you finally get your mother's attention. The cancer became a tragic "Competition for Love"—an unconscious attempt by Violeta's body to have a fate just as serious, just as heavy, and just as "worthy of grief" as Elena's. Her soul was crying out: *"Mother, look at me! I am suffering just like she is. Can you love me now?"*

Furthermore, the breast (systemically linked to nurturing) could be carrying the physical manifestation of the impossible, chronic burden: the inability to receive love and nurturing while being forced to be the constant emotional caretaker for her mother and the entire family system.

Breast Cancer Constellation

In one constellation, we focused directly on the symptom, setting up representatives for *Violeta, her cancer, her mother, and her recently deceased sister Elena.*

The movement was immediate and clarifying. As Elena's representative lay on the floor, the representative for the cancer was drawn strongly toward her, sitting down to look at her. This confirmed the hypothesis of Blind Loyalty. The cancer was acting as a mechanism for Violeta to follow her sister—a "longing to join the dead"—or, crucially, as an unconscious attempt to draw her grief-stricken mother's attention.

Since her mother was emotionally fixed on Elena's tragedy, Violeta's illness became a desperate, loyal cry for her mother's attention. Her body developed an equally serious fate (cancer) to align with Elena's gravity, hoping that by mirroring her sister's heavy fate, she would finally be seen and loved by her mother.

Releasing the Entanglement with Elena

The session focused on resolving the core entanglement between Violeta, her mother, and Elena, which was manifesting as a life-threatening systemic loyalty in Violeta's body. Our goal was to honor the loss and Elena's fate while freeing Violeta to live her own life by requesting her mother's blessing to separate.

Phase 1: Acknowledgment and Honoring the Mother's Bond

To initiate a systemic shift, we first acknowledged the reality of the mother's great love and grief. By acknowledging the mother's unique bond with Elena, we could begin to dissolve the unconscious competition for the mother's focus.

I asked Violeta to look at her mother's intense, ongoing bond with Elena and speak directly to her:

> **"Dear Mum, I really respect your love for Elena. I really want to give a place in my heart for your love for Elena."**

I then instructed her to bow and truly feel this acknowledgment.

Violeta responded with many tears, confirming the emotional power of this movement. As the acknowledgment settled in her soul, she reported a shift in the air: "I feel less emptiness between us, feel less cold and distant. I feel she still loves me, but she's still broken."

Phase 2: Defining the Boundary and Stating the Cost

The next step was addressing the dynamic of blind loyalty. Since the representative for the cancer had moved to sit next to Elena, it revealed Violeta was unconsciously trying to take her sister's place or follow her fate.

Intuitively, I asked Violeta to say to her mother:

"Dear Mum, it's too big for me to be both me and Elena at the same time. I don't want to do that anymore for myself either."

Then, we named the deadly price of this loyalty directly to her sister, bringing the "hidden contract" and cost to her life into the light:

"Dear Elena, it's costing me my life to bring you back."

Violeta cried deeply, realizing she was trying to bring Elena back for her mother at the expense of her own existence; but then had a profound realization as her soul snapped out of blind devotion: "It's true—I miss my sister, but the most I miss is how we felt as a family... the energy of love, joy. I miss you in all these feelings and it's costing me my life to bring you back for Mum as well."

Violeta paused, letting the weight of those words sink in. "I feel a sense of peace coming," she whispered. "I feel I have stopped wanting her to be back." By naming the cost, she was choosing the flow of her own life over the blind love that was consuming her.

Phase 3: Acceptance, Blessing, and Final Release

With the hidden contract exposed, we moved to the final, essential stage of healing: securing the Parental Blessing. This is the deep, felt permission from the parent for the child to live fully, even in the face of the family's tragedy. I guided Violeta to address her mother, not with guilt, but with the clarity of a child seeking freedom.

We started with the permission to lay down the burden she had carried out of love:

> **"Please look upon me with love Mama, out of love for you, I keep holding on to Elena, and it's costing me my life to continue loving you in this way.**
>
> **Please look upon me with love Mum, it's not my place to bring her back for you anymore.**
>
> **It's too big for a child to do this for a sad parent."**

As she spoke, Violeta stood up straighter, a visible wave of relief washing over her as she disentangled herself from her mother's burden.

To deepen the separation from her mother's grief, I asked her to say:

> **"Dear Mum, please look upon me with love if I let her go to the light and respect her destiny even if you still look for her or try and bring her back.**
>
> **Please look upon me with love if I look at her death with honor and respect and acceptance."**

Violeta breathed a deep sigh of relief. With her mother's burden released, Violeta turned to Elena. It was time to affirm her own right to life:

"Dear Elena, I respect who you are. I still miss you and give you a place in my heart even if I stay alive, please look upon me with love.

I will come only when it's my time to come as well."

This confirmed that Violeta was no longer bound by the unconscious contract to follow her sister into death. The representative for Elena then spoke: *"Please let me go, I need peace. Your grief keeps me holding on to you as well."*

Violeta responded immediately: *"I am letting her go, she needs to go."*

I then asked Violeta to bow to her sister and to her sister's destiny.

Then, sensing that her mother might never fully let go, she turned back to her and said:

"I respect your love for your daughter. Even if you join her, I want to respect this in my heart also."

As she spoke these words, her shoulders shook with the physical release of tension. She had freed herself from the impossible task of keeping her grieving mother happy. She finally understood it was time to live her own life, accepting her mother's path as the elder one.

To support Violeta's healing further, I also recommended a naturopathic protocol to strengthen her immunity and detoxify her body. This involved diet changes, gut healing protocols, liver detoxification herbs and lymphatic drainage remedies. If you would like to learn more about using naturopathic medicine and trauma healing to support your own healing journey, please watch my videos at www.drameet.com.

Restoring Freedom By Respecting Hierarchy

A year later, Violeta came for another retreat to Sardinia. She wanted to resolve her sense of burnout and overresponsibility. So I asked Violeta to choose representatives for *herself, her mother, her father, her 3 aborted siblings, her miscarried sibling, her sister who had just died, and her dead nephew.*

As Violeta watched her own constellation, she was surprised to see *how many siblings she had.* Both her representative and the representative of her mother were looking towards the floor, at the sister who just died. This sister lay in between Violeta and her mother, confirming Violeta's sense of isolation from her mother after her sister passed away.

Violeta loudly remarked *"This is how it is. The grief for my sister who died 3 years ago is an obstacle in our relationship. I feel that my mom is longing to join with my sister and dad who died."*

There seemed to be a lot of grief in the family. I had to work very carefully with each part of the constellation.

The Healing Movements

I wanted to focus on two primary movements: ***Restoring Hierarchy*** *and* ***Releasing her Mother's Grief***.

I asked Violeta to step into her own place in the constellation to speak the words that would restore the natural systemic order.

I intuitively chose three healing sentences for Violeta to speak, directly targeting the Hierarchy Imbalance and Blind Loyalty:

1. **Finding Her Place:**

    Initially, Violeta resisted accepting that she was the *sixth child* after all the abortions and miscarriage. So I asked her to explore a healing sentence that did not commit her to being the sixth child, but allowed her to experiment with the feeling of it. I got her to say to herself and her system:

    "It's ok to be the sixth and smallest kid from time to time."

    "I feel like a kid for the first time!" she remarked, as she felt the truth of the statement penetrate her nervous system.

    She smiled. She was slowly letting go of the burden of being the *"second child"* and allowed her childlike innocence to take over her body. We could all see the burden lift from her shoulders. *"Wow,"* she remarked, *"this feels so good"*. She finally gave herself the permission to be small and found her true place as the sixth child in her family.

2. **Restoring the Mother's Strength**

    It was now important to address the immense entanglement Violeta with her mother. To address the *imbalance of Hierarchy and Giving and Taking*, I first asked a representative for Violeta's grandmother to step in and stand behind Violeta's mother. I then asked Violeta to say out loud:

"I am not responsible for my mother's life, only for my own life. My mother has a mother, my Grandmother."

Violeta blinked a few times as she joyfully acknowledged her grandmother supporting her mother from behind. Her mother was no longer weak or needing her. She breathed a huge sigh of relief. She no longer had to be her mother's parent and the weight of her mother's life was safely in her mother's *and grandmother's authority*. Violeta was now free to live her own life as the child of her mother.

3. **Honoring the Mother's Longing**

Since Violeta's mother was still grieving for her dead daughter and husband, and Violeta was sad about the situation, I felt was time to heal the competition Violeta had with the deceased family members for her mothers love. The best way to do this was to honor her mother's love for the deceased. So I got Violeta to say to her mother:

"I am ready to let you go and I respect your longing for your husband and your daughter."

Violeta took a step back and breathed a huge sigh of relief. She suddenly felt profound peace and lightness in her heart as she separated from her mother's grief. She didn't have to stop her mother's grief anymore and it wasn't pulling her down anymore either. She was ready to live her own life with her own family. Without this important step, it was likely that Violeta had not been emotionally available to her own husband and children.

A few days later, Violeta happily wrote to me and said: *"I have found permission of living my own life, living my life for myself. I feel peace with my mother. Respecting my mother's wish as she is grieving and longing for the others. The feeling that I am not responsible for her life, it set me free. I resonated with "I am not your mother". I came to my womanhood for the first time. I feel joyful and light. I was able to turn my back to my family and face my life, for me, enjoying my life. I definitely feel that constellation shifted the energy because I have seen only playing kids on the plane to America. I haven't noticed them before."*

By respecting her mother's love for her dead sister, recognizing the role of her grandmother and acknowledging her four excluded siblings, Violeta was finally free to live the lighter life she was always meant to have.

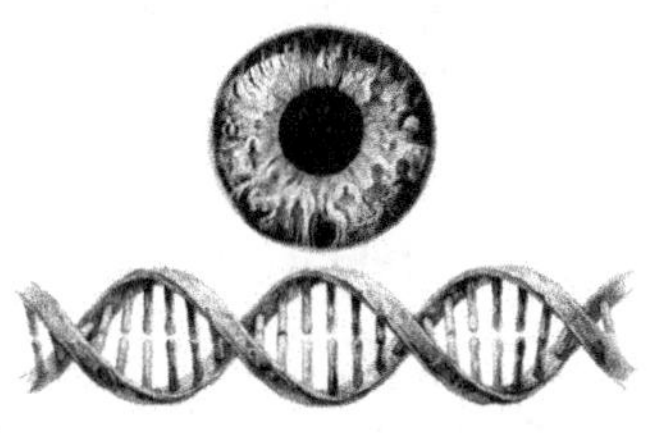

Chapter 12

Desire To Die To Save My Mother's Life

Dao, age 36, came in to see me with depression and strong feelings of wanting to die. She had suffered immense trauma rooted in extreme generational violence and abandonment.

Her life began with rejection and a desperate fight for survival: Dao's mother, pregnant with Dao at 18, was initially kicked out of her home by her own father (Dao's grandfather).

Dao's father was already involved with another woman who was also pregnant, and he became intensely abusive towards Dao's mother. He *kicked Dao's mother in her pregnant belly to try and abort Dao,* and forced her through both pill and surgical abortion attempts. Dao's mother recalled feeling "like dying" during this period. She believes Dao survived because, in her words, *"the surgeon wasn't able to find me"* and mum had *"prayed Lord Buddha a lot."*

In the constellation, it became apparent that Dao was entangled with her mother's trauma in two distinct and profound ways:

1. **Inherited Feeling:** She had inherited her mother's feelings of wanting to die, a deep sense of despair from the extreme violence her mother endured.
2. **Atonement/Sacrifice:** Dao had an *unconscious desire that if she dies, her mother's life would be saved.* This stemmed from the primal event where her mother's life was put in grave danger by the violent act of trying to abort Dao.

After Dao was born, her childhood was marked by violence and deep systemic fracture. Her father was abusive and used to hit her with a stick; his family rejected her because she was a girl. When Dao was three, Dao's mother left her with grandparents and uncles in Thailand to seek work in Europe. During this absence, when Dao was just three or four years old, she was sexually abused by her cousin in Thailand.

Later, when her mother returned and remarried, Dao endured further violence *from her own mother*, who carried her own legacy of abuse and suffered abuse from her own father (Dao's grandfather).

Because of this violence, Dao was tragically forced to seek emotional security from Dao's mother's new partner (*stepfather*). It was during this time, between the ages of 10 and 17, that the stepfather sexually abused her.

This situation led Dao to endure abuse from the person she relied on. The consequence of this forced reliance on her abuser likely created a profound psychological rift: it may have shattered Dao's ability to trust her own judgment and established a terrifying pattern where love and threat could become intrinsically linked *(trauma bonding)*, potentially fueling her later struggles with depression.

Healing Movements

Dao's work focused on shifting the weight of generational suffering and dismantling the psychological power her abusers held over her by asserting her own personal boundaries and destiny.

Releasing Inherited Emotions and the Sacrifice Contract

The first critical movement was separating Dao's identity from her mother's painful feelings of wanting to die. I asked Dao to try two healing sentences towards her mother:

"Dear mum, these are not all my feelings. Some of them are yours. Please forgive me if I let some of them go."

Dao blinked her eyes as she realized the immense emotional burden she was carrying for her mother. For the first time, she could clearly *distinguish her own feelings from those belonging to her suffering mother*, enabling her to release that heavy, inherited weight.

"Dear mum, even if I live, you can also live."

Dao breathed in a deep sigh of relief. She no longer had to die to save her mother's life. *"I no longer want to die,"* she slowly whispered to me.

Everyone in the room, including myself, had tears rolling down our cheeks as we witnessed tender Dao break through what had been years of suffering and painful thoughts. This healing sentence challenged Dao's old belief that she had to die for her mother to live, thereby freeing her from the unconscious contract of sacrifice.

Minimizing Abusers' Systemic Power and Reclaiming Life

This stage concluded Dao's previous movement by minimizing the systemic importance of the abusers and establishing Dao's personal sovereignty.

I suggested that Dao address her mother, establishing boundaries and personal choice. I intuitively chose the initial sentence to strip away the overwhelming *systemic weight and importance of the abusers* (Father, Stepfather, Cousin) by denying them the *elevated status* of "relative" and *the power that status implies*:

"Dear mom, these men are just men."

"Now I want to live my life as I want and die as I want."

She breathed in a deep sigh of relief, letting a huge burden go. The first sentence, referring to the abusers simply as **"just men,"** helped restore the autonomy, integrity, and individuality of the women in the family by minimizing the abusers' systemic power.

The second sentence empowered Dao by asserting that she does not have to die because some men wanted her to die. By asserting her right to own her life and destiny, Dao was able to release the entanglement with the men who wanted her to die.

Reconnecting with Father and Creating Safety

The next step of the constellation focused on re-including the father as the essential source of life while simultaneously ensuring Dao was no longer subservient or loyal to his previous abusive behaviour.

I asked Dao to say to the representative of her biological father:

"Dear dad, you are also my father, and I give you a place with men."

Dao stood up straighter as she reestablished the connection to her male lineage, and her voice became firmer as she distanced herself from her previous loyalty to the abuse in the family. She was now beginning to respect her own value and the importance of her own safety.

The core intervention here was the re-inclusion of the father as the source of life, overcoming the prior family rejection (including her mother's) of him. This enabled Dao to take the gift of her life completely. The second clause, **"I give you a place with men,"** effectively demoted his status. By choosing to relinquish the loyalty tied to the imagined, elevated status of "Father," it became far easier for Dao to let go of the loyalty to the abuse as a "obedient daughter", thereby claiming back her autonomy.

I then guided Dao to assert her personal boundary and right to safety:

"I have the right to protect myself."

Dao nodded in agreement with herself, drawing a deep breath of confirmation. In this final, powerful shift, she re-established her authority over her safety, directly countering the lifelong systemic message that her body and boundaries were violable. This affirmation drew a clear internal boundary, allowing her to stand firmly in her sovereignty and move forward, no longer feeling so vulnerable to abuse.

The Journey Forward

This moment marked the true beginning of Dao's return to self. Though mountains of work remained, the deep roots of her distress - the silent chains of unconscious family loyalties - had been tenderly undone. The ancestral weight was gone, making the continuation of her healing journey a path of grace, allowing her to fully receive the benefits of ongoing therapy.

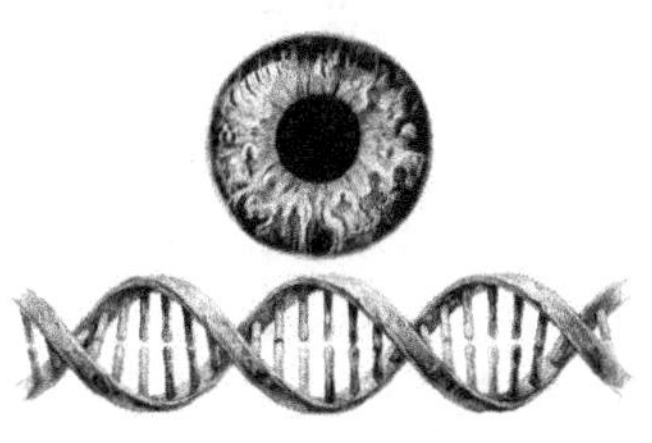

Chapter 13

Hip Pain: Mary Loves Her Husband

Mary, a 49-year-old woman, came to Kenya for chronic **left hip pain** that had plagued her for years, severely impacting her daily well-being. The pain's onset was significant: it began shortly after her marriage to John, a man from a different cultural background.

Mary's symptom - the chronic hip pain – seemed to be correlated with her marriage, suggesting a systemic entanglement rooted in the new family system. Mary revealed that her marriage to John was met with resistance and rejection from John's family due to their differing cultural backgrounds. This disapproval created emotional strife that deeply affected both Mary and her husband.

Systemically, Mary's hip pain seemed to be an unconscious physical entanglement: she absorbed the emotional burden and strife of her husband, John. As the body's center for support and movement, the hip registered her loyalty and desire to "carry" him through his family's rejection by mirroring his emotional pain as a physical load.

Constellation Process and Healing Movements

The constellation included representatives for Mary, John, and John's family members. As the dynamics unfolded, it became clear that Mary had entangled herself with John's feelings of rejection.

I guided Mary to say a specific sentence to her husband in order to challenge her nervous system to register whether this act of loyalty was truly supporting her own life or interfering with it, thereby bringing this entanglement into the light:

"I will bear this burden with you."

While this statement expresses immense loyalty and love, in the systemic context, it revealed Mary's profound commitment to absorbing his pain. It helped Mary become fully aware of how she had involuntarily taken on her husband's strife and the rejection he felt from his family.

Mary blinked and shifted as she realized her blind loyalty was not helping anyone. This newfound awareness provided a pivotal turning point. It allowed Mary to perform the essential systemic movement: separating her husband's burdens and his family's rejection from her own nervous system and heart.

"I feel a relief throughout my body and even feel sensations in my hip and lower back", she said, slightly amazed.

A week later, when I asked how she was carrying on, Mary reported a significant improvement in her chronic hip pain. The emotional burden she had been carrying had been a major contributing factor to her physical discomfort. By letting go of the stress to "fix" or carry John's family strife, Mary not only experienced relief from her chronic hip pain but also felt a deeper, healthier connection and role in her own nuclear family now.

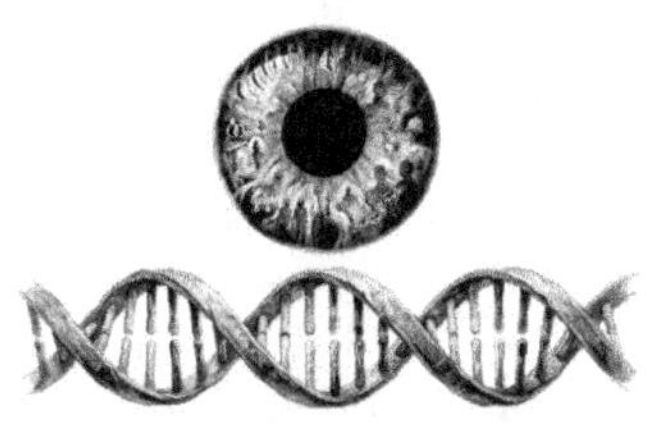

Chapter 14

Relationships: Holocaust Survivor's Guilt & Inge

Inge came to one of my retreats in Sardinia, looking for a way forward with recurring life challenges. As is my practice, I asked her to pause and move past the intellectual request to discover the deepest intention of her heart. After a moment of quiet reflection, she voiced her focus.

"I want to explore how my family history may be affecting me, and I'd also like to find a truly loving relationship and not be with someone who won't be with me wholly."

I then asked Inge about her family history. She said:

"My Grandfather had been Jewish and fled Berlin back in 1937. His three sisters were later gassed in the camps and his mother committed suicide by jumping out of a building on the eve of her assigned transport to a concentration camp. He had tried to convince them to leave Germany when he left but they didn't believe it would be bad, and when they changed their minds the US would not give them visas. He carried this devastating survivor's guilt and a crushing grief because he had tried to get them to leave, only to be stopped by those awful visa restrictions when they finally agreed."

Her Constellation

So I set up the constellation with representatives for:

- Inge
- Maternal Grandfather
- Maternal Grandmother
- The three Aunts (who were murdered)
- The War itself (personified)

Inge's representative was fixated on her Grandfather. The three Aunts and the Grandmother immediately lay on the floor, revealing that their tragic death was lingering in Inge's system. The Grandfather was staring at his dead relatives on the floor, unable to move.

Since the energy of this systemic pull was very strong, I asked Inge to step into the constellation instead of her representative. She was immediately drawn to her Grandfather and expressed profound sadness for his loss, and was moved to crying.

Her focus, and that of the Grandfather's representative, was fixed upon the Aunts and the representative of The War. This movement visually confirmed the entanglement: Inge was standing in a position of shared burden and grief alongside her Grandfather, identifying with his profound loss instead of fully occupying her place as a *granddaughter.*

The systemic principle at play here is that unintegrated trauma and unresolved grief - especially those involving death, exclusion, or major historical events like the Holocaust - can be carried by later generations out of *Blind Loyalty.* This unconscious loyalty binds the descendant (Inge) to the ancestor's fate, making it difficult or impossible for her to fully choose or commit to her *own* life and love, as that would unconsciously *betray* her ancestors' suffering.

Healing Movements

The crucial movement was to release Inge from the burden of her Grandfather's unintegrated grief and restore the Order of Love (the fundamental systemic principle of hierarchy). To shift the entanglement, the therapeutic focus moved from the loss to the relationship between Inge and her Grandfather.

I felt the first step was to give dignity back to her grandfather for his difficult life path. So I asked Inge to face her Grandfather and say:

"Grandfather I honor your fate…"

Inge took a step back and relaxed. She had spoken the language of acceptance, not judgment or correction.

Then, to re-establish the systemic hierarchy and encourage Inge to return the *weight* of the trauma to the rightful carrier, the elder, and step back into her "light" position as the youngest, I asked her to say:

"I give the responsibility for your loss and sadness back to you. I am only a child. You are the Grandpa. This is not mine to carry…"

Inge relaxed into herself a bit more. She had severed her unconscious identification with her grandfather's grief.

The final step was to somatically feel the permission to live her life and separate her destiny from her ancestor's loss and grief. I asked her to request permission from her grandfather by saying:

"Please allow me to live my life fully..."

After Inge spoke these words, the representative for The War reported that she felt *the energy of the war had left her* and that her presence was no longer required, before slowly moving out of the constellation.

Inge herself said she felt much more centered and able to fully embody her own life.

The diminishing and departure of "The War" demonstrated the successful release of the systemic energy that had been driving her unconscious commitment to loss and avoidance of deep, fulfilling connection as solely the *Grandchild*. By returning the burden, she was able to embody her *correct position in her family system* and was more free to choose a fulfilling life for *herself.*

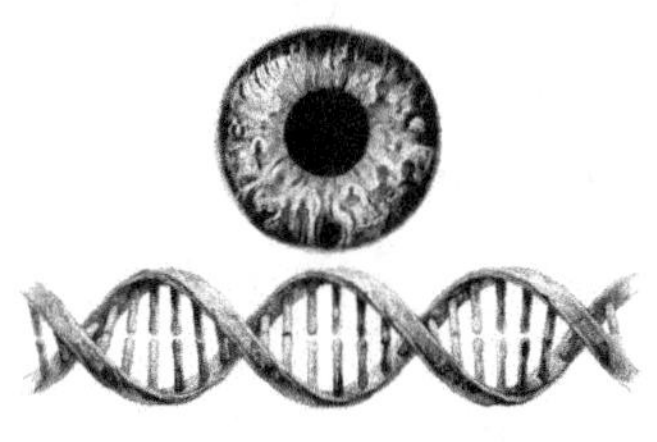

Chapter 15

Loneliness: Margarida's Absent Parents

Margarida felt unloved and disconnected from her parents. Her parents' absence was rooted in their powerful, unresolved entanglements with the histories and losses of their own families of origin, a dynamic that ultimately led to their divorce. Margarida's struggle was compounded by the subtle systemic weight of an unacknowledged miscarried sibling who came directly before her. Margarida was living life with the responsibility of a *second* child in her family, rather than taking her place as the *third* child in her system.

History and Context: Intergenerational Burden and Loss

Margarida's systemic pattern involved multiple layers of ancestral and nuclear family trauma:

1. Maternal Lineage: The Heavy Cost of an Unwilling Arrival

The journey of Margarida's mother began not in celebration, but in resistance. She was born before her parents were married, and her father (GF-m) had been clear he did not want children. The marriage only took place because Margarida's Mother was already on her way. This circumstance placed an invisible but heavy *relational burden* on her, a feeling of being an obligation rather than a gift. Later, following her and her sister (MS), the maternal grandmother (GM-m) had three abortions. These *unacknowledged, excluded siblings* cast a long shadow, creating a deep *systemic sadness*. They were the children who never were, and their unmourned existence left Margarida's Mother feeling heavy and unsure of her own right to fully take her place.

2. Paternal Lineage: The Draining Weight of Premature Grief

Margarida's Father was forced to grow up far too quickly. His own father (GF-f) passed away when Margarida's Father was young, and in the absence of a father figure, he took on an immense responsibility, becoming a surrogate parent to his younger brother. He looked after him *like a son*, and this profound, premature role completely consumed Margarida's Father's emotional energy. He simply had no emotional resources left to be a father to Margarida when she arrived. The pattern of sorrow repeated when that younger brother passed away, resulting in devastating, unintegrated grief that overwhelmed him. Margarida's Father's entire being became absorbed in this loss, making him completely unavailable to both Margarida and Margarida's Mother (his wife).

Systemic Diagnosis: Blocked Flow and Loyalty Entanglement

Margarida's current dynamic was a consequence of these historical blocks:

1. *Blocked Parental Flow:* Both Margarida's Mother and Margarida's Father were psychologically tethered to their pasts and their families of origin, preventing them from being present in their marital relationship or with Margarida.

   o *Margarida's Mother's Bond:* To her birth circumstance and the unacknowledged abortions.
   o *Margarida's Father's Bond:* To the grief over his father and the loss of his brother.

2. *Relational Exclusion:* Since Margarida's Mother and Margarida's Father were internally preoccupied by their family tragedies, they were not emotionally available to one another or to Margarida.

3. *Margarida's Parents' Divorce:* The eventual divorce was a systemic reflection of their primary emotional loyalty lying outside the marital bond. Margarida was left without the necessary emotional support from two present parents.

Initial Constellation Setup

I set up a constellation to expose the key emotional blockages and hidden loyalties influencing Margarida.

Role (Margarida's Perception)	Representative	Initial Position / Key Dynamic
Margarida	Client Representative	Standing slightly apart, showing a subtle leaning towards the Lost Sibling's space.
Margarida's Mother	Mother Representative	Heavy and withdrawn, subtly looking away from Margarida's Father and towards the empty space representing aborted siblings.

Role (Margarida's Perception)	Representative	Initial Position / Key Dynamic
Margarida's Father	Father Representative	Heavy and emotionally distant, focused on the space representing his Deceased Brother.

Healing Movements

Margarida's process focused on acknowledging the excluded, validating the burdens, and re-establishing the correct hierarchy, beginning with Margarida's rightful place.

Phase 1: Restoring Margarida's Place and Acknowledging the Lost Sibling

To properly place Margarida as the third child in her family, I asked a representative to lie on the floor in the position of the miscarried sibling. I then got Margarida to take the place of her own representative and address her sibling and parents directly.

- I got Margarida to say to the missing child on the floor:

  "I see you now. You are the second child, and you belong here. I give you a place in my heart."

  - *Effect:* Margarida reported feeling a profound relief, as if a long-carried burden had lifted, and she felt suddenly more free in her body.

- I then got Margarida to face her parents and say:

  "I cannot be the second child anymore. I take my true

place. I am the third child. Please see me and bless me as the third child."

- o *Effect:* The representatives of the parents nodded in agreement and Margarida started to feel more congruent in her body and more at peace with herself.

Phase 2: Accepting the Mother and Releasing the Maternal Burden

As Margarida began to feel more secure in her process, I focused on helping Margarida connect with her parents in a different way. I first focused on freeing Margarida's Mother from her generational entanglements.

Because her mother's representative was still focused on the empty space of her aborted siblings, I got three representatives to lie on the floor to represent the aborted children. I also got a representative for Margarida's maternal Grandmother (GM-m) to stand in the circle.

I then had the mother's representative lie next to her aborted siblings to see what would happen. Slowly, she began to weep tears of sorrow as she started to feel their presence and the profound loss in the family.

As the tears subsided, she looked towards her mother (GM-m), who was still fixated on the aborted siblings. You could see that Margarida's mother was craving for her mother to connect with her. To help free her from this *systemic competition* with her siblings, and become more available to her living family (Margarida), I asked Margarida's Mother to say to her own mother (GM-m):

"I respect your love for your children and my siblings."

Effect: You could immediately see the mother's representative *relax* and let go of an entanglement with the grandmother's absence. She was now more free and stood up and faced Margarida with love. Margarida took a deep sigh of relief as she realized her mother had also lacked emotional support as a child, and could not have possibly learnt to give differently to her.

I gently asked Margarida to say to her mother:

"I respect your love for your mother and your siblings. You are the perfect mother for me. And I've missed you…"

Effect: You could see Margarida's heart crack open as tears rolled down her cheeks - a clear sign of honesty and connection. With love, Margarida and her mother slowly embraced, Margarida's body relaxing into her mother's body, finally feeling her sense of belonging.

Phase 3: Releasing the Paternal Grief and Taking Life from Father

With Margarida now having cleared her mother's field, she took the final step to acknowledge her father's grief and loyalty, letting go of the pain of his absence and stepping out of competition with his past entanglements.

I asked Margarida to face her father and say:

"I respect your love for your father and brother."

Margarida felt a deep calmness wash over her, noting that the tension in her chest related to her father's distance was starting to ease. Once again, she realized that her father also didn't have the emotional support he needed growing up, and that he could not have been any different for her.

Why I used these healing sentences...

The phrases **"I respect your love for your..."** and **"You are the perfect mother/father for me"** are essential healing movements that facilitate *reconciliation and unconditional acceptance* within the child, driving a systemic shift:

1. **"I respect your love for your..." honors loyalty and ends competition:**

   This sentence *validates and honors the primary emotional loyalty and sorrow* that preoccupied both parents, which was the source of their unavailability. Traditionally, a child might resent her parents' preoccupation. By showing this respect, Margarida *steps out of competition* with those excluded figures. This releases the parents from the unconscious debt of having to be "more present" to her, allowing them to turn toward her freely.

   Paradoxically, the validation and honoring of their burdens allows both parents to shed their unconscious roles (e.g., the mother's struggle to fully "take her place," the father's role as "griever/surrogate parent"). This frees the parents' systems to step fully into their proper roles as husband, wife, and present parents to Margarida, strengthening the relational triangle.

2. **"You are the perfect mother/father for me"**: This is the moment of unconditional acceptance, meaning, *"I take you exactly as you are - with all your flaws and sadnesses."* The child relinquishes the entitled expectation that the parent should have been different. By accepting the perfect parent

she received, Margarida takes her life gift without condition, which is the foundational step for her to fully thrive.

Resolution: Taking Her Place and Moving Forward

With both parents having addressed their past and recognized Margarida in her correct place, I closed the circle by helping Margarida fully accept her life and move toward her future.

I asked Margarida to notice how she felt as she looked at both parents now. She softly said: *"I feel like I belong in a family now."*

After she said this, I asked her to bow to both her parents and thank them for their gift of life. Margarida did so, and you could see her surrender to something bigger than herself – *The innate love of her parents...*

Finally, I got Margarida to face a direction that represented her life. As she did this, I got both parents to stand behind her, and put their hands on Margarida's shoulders as a symbol of parental support.

Margarida smiled and stood up taller. She finally felt the connection to her ancestral lineage, which gave her strength to be herself and move forward in life with more self esteem and certainty.

This transformative shift occurs because the child's strength, inner certainty, and capacity to thrive come from successfully *"taking both parents"*, who act as conduits for the ancestral life force. By clearing the blocked flow caused by their past burdens, the energy now flows freely to Margarida. This deep, internal reconciliation grants her an innate sense of security, and allows her to stand strong in her own life.

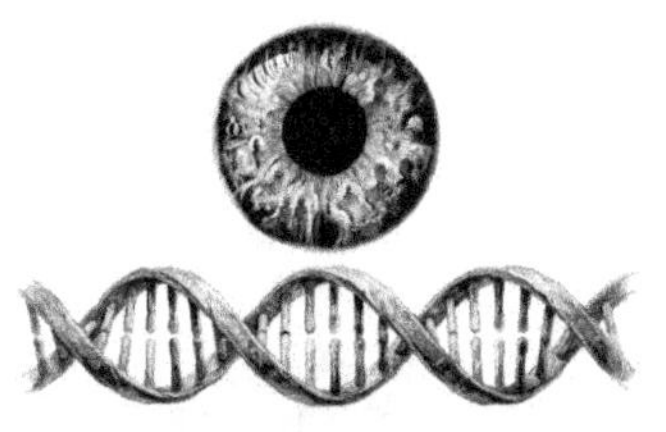

Chapter 16

Knee Pain & Accidents: Catalin Follows Father

Catalin was a young man plagued by a persistent pattern of physical issues: severe stiffness in one knee and a series of recurring annual accidents. The accidents were particularly concerning as they happened around the same time each year. His systemic symptom was this annual, self-sabotaging pattern of injury and restriction.

Phase 1: The Initial Image and Diagnosis

I began by asking Catalin when this pattern started. He reported, "about 5 years ago." When asked what happened around that time, he responded that his father had passed away then, and that he was very close to him.

I thought to myself that Catalin's recurring pattern was an unconscious entanglement stemming from his grief for his beloved father.

Staging the Constellation

I set up the constellation simply with representatives for Catalin and his Father.

Representative	Initial Position & Observation	Possible Systemic Meaning
Catalin	Stood intensely drawn toward his Father's representative; rigid posture.	**Unconscious identification with the dead**; attempting to follow his father's fate out of love and grief.
Father	Stood still, appearing to receive Catalin's focus.	Representing the deceased, the anchor of the entanglement.

The key observation was Catalin's intense, almost magnetically **drawn connection** to his father. Systemically, it is common for children who were very close to a deceased parent to manifest disease, accidents, or life restrictions in an unconscious attempt to "join" the parent in death.

Phase 2: Systemic Entanglement and The Core Block

The core of the issue was Catalin's systemic entanglement: an unconscious, strong loyalty to his deceased father that compelled him to share his father's fate. This commitment to the past and to death, rather than to his own vitality and the future, created the Systemic Block. His stiff knee and recurring annual accidents were physical manifestations of this inner conflict, acting as a "brake on his life" and blocking the natural flow of movement and life force.

To break this life-limiting identification, I had Catalin look at his father's representative and say a sentence of separation and affirmation of his own life:

"I will join you when it's my time, not before."

The effect was immediate: you could see something change in Catalin's eyes, and the father's representative also seemed relieved. This systemic movement acknowledged the bond while clearly stating Catalin's commitment to life.

Phase 3: Restoration of the Life Flow

With Catalin's unconscious pull toward death released, the next movement focused on accepting his gift of life and activating his personal power and purpose.

I guided Catalin through an act of honor and gratitude, having him bow to his father and say:

"Thank you for giving me life, I take this gift from you in my heart."

You could see Catalin relax as he connected with his own sense of self and purpose in life. He was no longer drawn to following his father's fate and was now free to live his own life. In systemic terms, this sentence restores the **Order of Giving and Taking**, where the child honors the greatest gift (life) received from the parent, which solidifies their right to live fully.

Phase 4: Integration and Conclusion

During the constellation, Catalin reported that *his knee felt freer*, and he felt a palpable *permission to move forward in life*. This physical change directly correlated with the systemic shift, as the knee often symbolizes a person's ability to move forward in their life.

A year later, Catalin returned for another retreat. He was extremely happy with the results of his last constellation. I personally was a bit surprised with what he reported, especially about accidents:

- He reported that he had no issues with his knees anymore.
- He was no longer prone to accidents and was living a much happier life.

The strange pattern of annual injury, which was possibly a hidden loyalty to follow his father, had surprisingly ceased as the underlying systemic entanglement of the **Identification with the Dead** had been respectfully resolved.

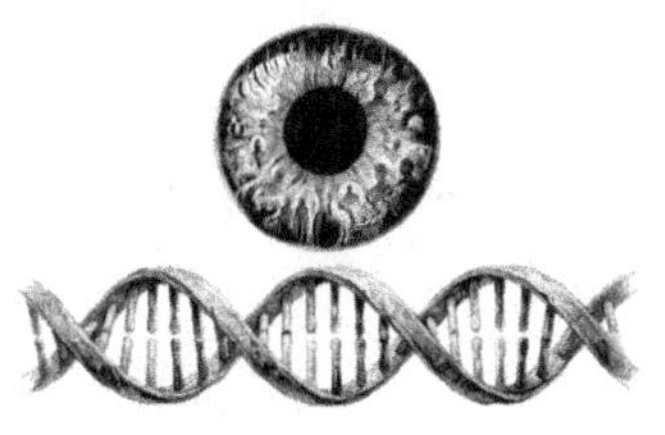

Chapter 17

Burnout & Anxiety: War & Exile For Henrietta's Father

Henrietta, a woman in her 30s with a gentle but weary presence, came to me seeking relief from a life defined by crippling exhaustion and a relentless, driving anxiety. Despite her professional success, she felt like an overachiever running on empty, unable to escape a deep-seated need to "fix" everything around her.

Her medical history told a story of its own: at just eighteen, she had battled lymphoma. The subsequent radiation therapy had left her with hypothyroidism, a permanent physical slowing of the body that seemed to mirror her internal state of burnout.

When we looked into her past, we found that the seeds of her exhaustion weren't sown in her adulthood, but in the soil of Iraq—a land of ancient beauty and modern tragedy.

The Systemic Root: War, Displacement, and the "Take Me First" Prayer

Henrietta's childhood was shaped by the terrifying uncertainty of war. For a child, the world is only as safe as their parents are. When the external world becomes a landscape of sirens and danger, the child's focus narrows intensely onto the mother and father.

Henrietta shared a memory that revealed the depth of her childhood burden: *"Growing up in Iraq amidst ongoing war, I developed a profound fear of losing my parents. I vividly remember praying as a child, asking God to take me first because I couldn't bear the thought of life without them."*

This prayer, while born of love, carries a heavy systemic weight. It is not an offer of sacrifice to save them, but rather a reflection of the child's absolute dependency—an admission that her own life had no meaning or safety without their presence. By asking to be "taken first," her soul was making a preemptive exit from a world she couldn't imagine facing alone. This "blind love" creates a deep vulnerability in the body; when a child's heart is so tethered to the potential loss of their parents, the soul becomes partially "turned toward death," leaving very little energy for the vital, forward-looking task of growing into one's own life.

When the war forced her family to flee their ancestral home, the trauma of displacement fell heavily on her father. He was a man who loved his land, his heritage, and his roots. To leave was to lose his identity. Henrietta watched his silent suffering with an agonizing sorrow:

"I had clear memories of the struggles he experienced and I felt so sorry for him. It was gut wrenching to imagine what he must have experienced when he decided that it was time for us to leave the country. Often times, my heart would be full of pain and sorrow looking back at those specific childhood memories."

The "Fixer" and the Parentified Child

Because her father was paralyzed by his own grief and unable to express his feelings, Henrietta unconsciously stepped out of her place as the child and into the role of his emotional caretaker. This is what we call **Parentification**.

Out of a desperate desire for safety and affection, Henrietta tried to "save" her father from his pain. If she could be perfect, if she could overachieve, if she could carry his sorrow for him, then perhaps he would be okay—and then, finally, she would be safe. This internal pressure to "fix" a parent's life is a primary driver of adult burnout and chronic anxiety. You cannot fix the past, and you cannot carry a parent's fate without eventually collapsing under the weight.

Resolution and Systemic Healing

Our work focused on a singular, powerful movement: allowing Henrietta to put down the heavy mantle of the "mother" and return to the safety of being the "child."

Step 1: Releasing the Mothering Role

To break the cycle of over-responsibility, Henrietta needed to consciously acknowledge the boundary she had crossed. I guided her to look at the image of her father and speak the simple, difficult truth that her soul needed to hear:

> **"I'm not Dad's mother." "I'm not his mother and it's good for me to see that."**

The shift was instantaneous. Henrietta breathed a sigh that seemed decades in the making. *"It is less pressure to be the child,"* she whispered. *"I like it. It makes me feel safe."*

For the first time since the war began, she didn't have to be the guardian of her father's heart.

Step 2: Respecting the Father's Private Grief

In the constellation, we discovered another layer. Henrietta's father was energetically "pulled" toward his brother. Often, when a parent is emotionally unavailable, it is because they are "looking" at someone who was lost or excluded in their own generation.

Instead of competing with the brother for her father's attention, Henrietta needed to respect her father's right to his own relationships and his own grief. This is a movement of humility—acknowledging that a parent has a life and a heart that belongs to others besides the child.

I asked her to say to her father:

"I know you love your brother and I respect your love for him."

By honoring his bond with his brother, Henrietta stopped trying to be her father's "everything." She gave him back his adulthood.

Step 3: The Father's Truth

As Henrietta stepped back into her place as the "small one," the representative for her father was finally able to speak. The "strong, silent" mask fell away, revealing the love that had been trapped behind his trauma:

"I'm not as strong as everyone thinks I am so I couldn't show you love, but I have a lot of love for you. Let me have my own grief and connection."

Hearing this allowed Henrietta to finally see her father as a human being—limited, grieving, but deeply loving. She didn't need him to be perfect to feel his love. She felt a profound sense of "settling" and completeness. Her sense of self-worth was no longer tied to how much of his pain she could carry, but was now anchored in the simple, quiet security of knowing how deeply she was loved by him.

Testing Her Resolution

To ensure the healing had taken root, I asked Henrietta to try on her old "heavy" thoughts: *"I am responsible for you, Dad. This is my burden."*

She shook her head, a light smile on her face. *"These phrases don't align with how I am feeling. I no longer associate with them. I realize the healing has taken place."*

A year later, the transformation was evident. The "fixer" had finally found rest. Henrietta reported: *"Now when I replay those memories of my father from the time we had to leave Iraq, I no longer feel responsible for him or feel sad for him. I feel great love for him, but the burden is gone. I feel lighter... I no longer feel compelled to fix everything for everyone or to carry their pain.*

The family constellation experience has profoundly shifted my perspective and brought me a newfound peace. I remain amazed by the love and support I received and wholeheartedly recommend family constellation for anyone healing from childhood trauma."

By returning her father's fate to him, Henrietta finally gave herself permission to live. The exhaustion of the "Take me first" prayer was replaced by the peace of a woman who is finally, safely, the child of her parents.

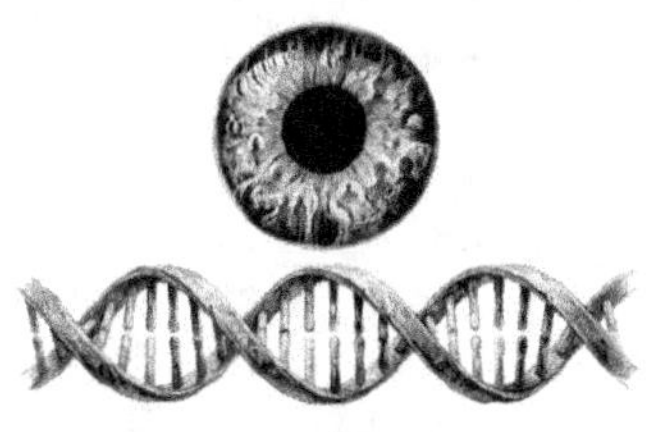

Chapter 18

Resentment: Karen's Mother & Father Abandoned

K aren was a beautiful innocent human being who came to my retreat with an issue I see quite often: she was carrying deep conflict and judgment toward her father, who had left her mother for a second wife. Her symptom was a severe loyalty entanglement to her grieving mother, which prevented her from reconnecting with her father.

Phase 1: The Initial Image and Diagnosis

Staging the Immediate Family

I first set up the constellation with representatives for Karen, Mother, and Father.

Representative	Initial Position & Observation	Possible Systemic Meaning
Karen	Stood close to Mother, facing Father with a rigid, cold posture.	Fierce loyalty to Mother; blocking the father-daughter bond.

Representative	Initial Position & Observation	Possible Systemic Meaning
Mother	Slumped, not looking at Father or Karen.	Feeling unsupported in life, grieving the marriage, and carrying the emotional fallout of the separation.
Father	Stood far away, looking lost, with no clear place in the system.	Rejected by the original family unit; exiled by Karen's judgment.

Introducing the Ancestral Block

I then brought in representatives for the Mother's parents, the Grandmother (GM) and Grandfather (GF), to understand the source of the Mother's deep unresolved pain.

Representative	Position & Observation	Possible Systemic Meaning
Grandmother (GM)	Stood apart from Mother, facing an empty space in front of her.	Entangled in unresolved grief, likely for dead children.
Grandfather (GF)	Stood slightly behind GM, and looking away from Mother.	Cannot truly see Mother, as his attention is blocked by GM's entanglement with her missing children.

The first observation confirmed the hidden dynamic: Karen's Mother's pain was fundamentally about a multi-generational pattern of being unseen and unsupported, starting with her own mother's (GM's) unresolved grief.

Phase 2: Uncovering the Ancestral Entanglement

I asked Karen about her Grandmother's history, and Karen confirmed that her Grandmother had suffered three miscarriages. Two miscarriages were before Karen's mother was born, and one after she was born. I then focused on Karen's Grandmother (GM) and her position facing the empty space. When asked about her feelings, Karen's GM representative expressed an overwhelming grief and an inability to move.

Her heart was with the others (the miscarried children), and she was not able to look at her living daughter (Karen's Mother).

This confirmed the core issue: Karen's GM was so entangled with the grief for the dead children that her heart remained closed to her living daughter. This violated the Order of Precedence - a fundamental systemic law where the *needs of the living child always take priority over the dead.* By focusing all her energy on the past, the GM unintentionally created an emotional vacuum around Karen's Mother.

To bring the family's unspoken grief into expression, I asked a representative to lie on the floor to represent the miscarried children. I then asked Karen's GM representative to kneel on the floor next to her miscarried children. As Karen's GM representative took this position, she immediately burst into tears, finally able to fully grieve them and bring the forgotten souls and her own sadness into the system's awareness.

The representative for the Mother expressed a deep *fatigue.* She was subconsciously *identifying with* and taking on the emotional "place" of the miscarried children, hoping that by standing where her mother (GM) was focused, she would finally be *seen* by her mother (GM). This unconscious dynamic occurs because children sometimes identify with the person who is excluded or the issue upon which their loved one (especially their parent) is focused. By identifying with what has their loved one's attention, the child *attempts to be better seen* by the person who has been looking away from them.

Marital Strain Hypothesis: Since the Mother was unconsciously identifying with the dead (miscarried children), she was systemically and emotionally unavailable to those in her own life, including her husband (Karen's Father). This lack of full presence would have created a deep emotional distance in the marriage, possibly leading the husband to seek the warmth and affection he lacked elsewhere, thereby contributing significantly to the separation.

Phase 3: The Resolution and Flow of Support

The therapeutic movement was to restore the proper flow of love, starting with the oldest generation.

As Karen's GM representative was now able to process her grief fully on the floor, she slowly turned. When she finally looked at her daughter (Karen's Mother), the Mother's representative wept uncontrollably, expressing a lifetime of feeling unseen. Both GM and Mother were drawn to each other to embrace, establishing the first true emotional connection to a parent for the Mother.

Next, Karen's Grandfather's (GF) representative *immediately* moved closer to Karen's Mother.

The systemic principle at work here is that a *father often connects to his child through the mother.* Because Karen's Grandmother (GM) had been emotionally blocked from seeing her daughter, Karen's Grandfather (GF) could not fully connect either. Once Karen's GM opened the channel of love and finally embraced her daughter, Karen's GF was automatically drawn in and could *accept his child*

(Karen's Mother) fully. His connection restored the complete parental support Karen's Mother had always missed.

Phase 4: Karen's Disentanglement and Reconciliation

With her Mother finally seen and supported by her own parents, the burden on Karen lifted. The Mother's representative stood taller and looked at Karen with strength for the first time.

Karen immediately relaxed her rigid shoulders and her gaze softened toward her Father. She was now able to let go of rescuing or protecting her Mother, and was able to reconcile her separation with her Father in an easier way. The reconciliation was only possible after Karen's mother had connected to her parents (GM and GF) because the systemic burden of the Mother - the fear that she would "fall apart" if Karen dared to connect with the Father - had been returned to the Mother's parents.

I asked Karen to say to her mother:

"I am only your daughter. I leave what is yours with you. Please bless me if I look towards father again with love."

She took a step back and breathed a sigh of relief. This separation allowed Karen to see her Father as simply her Father, rather than an enemy she had to punish out of loyalty to her Mother's pain. The chronic loyalty entanglement was broken. I then guided Karen through the final reconciliation with her Father. I asked her to say:

"I am your daughter. I take you in completely as you are. I'm always your daughter."

Karen commented that she felt less resistant about meeting her father again. The constellation image ended with Karen facing her Father directly, ready to reconnect, and her Mother standing strong and supported by her own parents. Karen was now free to accept the Father's love, along with his choice of his new wife.

Anger & Relationship Reversal: Aria Is Only A Child

Aria, the eldest of three siblings, came to me because she had always felt a deep, exhausting need to fight for her place in the family. She was also extremely angry towards her grandfather. Furthermore, Aria was often arguing with her mother and protecting her father, which stressed her even more.

Her issues were tied to a difficult family history: her maternal grandfather struggled with alcoholism and died of lung cancer, and her grandmother passed away from breast cancer at a young age. The grandfather's alcoholism had made it difficult for Aria's mother to connect with him, a dynamic that can often put an unconscious expectation on her partner (Aria's father) to fill that empty relational role.

Healing Movements

Disentangling the Aunt's Anger

I felt Aria's anger towards her grandfather *was disproportionate to her role* in the family, suggesting an inherited burden. To investigate, I set up representatives for her mother and her siblings (Aria's maternal aunt being one of them).

In the constellation, *Aria's maternal aunt,* was furious at the grandfather's representative. It was obvious whose anger Aria was carrying. This was the first critical entanglement. I asked Aria what happened with her Aunt and Aria said: *"It's true, my aunt was very angry with my grandfather because he didn't take my grandmother to hospital in time, and she died of breast cancer."*

So I asked Aria to face the representative of her aunt and separate this inherited emotional burden by asking her to say:

"I honor your story, dear Aunty, but I leave your destiny to you."

Aria felt relieved. She hadn't realized that she had been carrying anger on behalf of her aunt. She then looked over to her grandfather and bowed her head slowly, allowing a sense of peace to fill her heart towards him. I allowed her to feel her true place in her family as just his granddaughter, and not a child who was carrying a heavy burden.

Dissolving the Maternal Dynamic

Once her inherited anger was cleared, I focused on Aria's relationship with her parents. Her representative often moved to stand near her father, looking at him with deep support, which is typical of the way a mother would support a child. I felt Aria had unconsciously stepped into the role of being her father's mother (her grandmother), becoming his primary emotional support system whenever conflict arose with her actual mother.

When a man has an unfulfilled need for maternal connection, protection, or validation from his own mother, he may unconsciously seek that missing role fulfillment from his daughter.

In these cases, the daughter becomes the "little mother" to her father. She feels responsible for his happiness and emotional stability, which effectively ousts her own mother from her rightful place as the father's partner. This "parentification" of the child is a heavy burden; by mothering her father, Aria was essentially making herself "bigger" than both her parents, which caused conflict between her and her mother and prevented her from receiving the care she actually needed. Noticing this, I asked Aria to step into her representative place and respectfully say to her father:

"I love you, but I am your daughter, not your mother."

As she said this, Aria felt a sense of relief and took a step back from her father as she released this exhausting burden. She then automatically gazed towards her mother as a young child. She was no longer in competition with her mother or identifying with her father's mother. She could finally take in her mother as just the child.

I asked her to walk towards her mother and kneel before her as a child. She wept softly, realizing how much she had missed her mother's love all these years. I gave Aria some time to feel this new connection and absorb all her mother's love as a young child. As she did this, her nervous system began transforming, rewriting parts of her emotional history with her parents.

A year later, Aria wrote to me and said: *"It is changing my life and the way I look at my family. Thank you for those intensive days. Grateful for turning me upside down because that's how I began to understand my direction."*

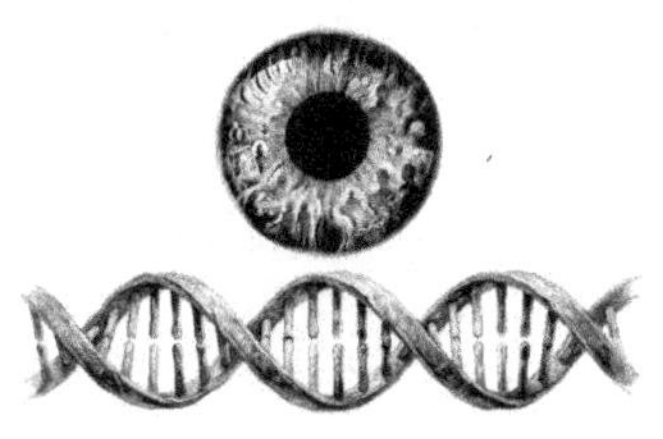

Chapter 19

Sexual Abuse & Isolation: Daniel's Grandfathers & War

Daniel arrived at the retreat carrying a heavy shroud of isolation and a deep-seated shame that had colored his entire adult life. He described a persistent depression and a feeling of being "adrift" within his own family. His history was one of profound fragmentation and silence.

When Daniel was four, his mother fled South America for Europe—a move made for her own survival that necessitated a total cutoff from Daniel's father and the entire maternal extended family. At age eleven, in the midst of this upheaval, Daniel experienced a traumatic sexual abuse event by an eighteen-year-old cousin. Because his mother was consumed by her own survival and the secret of a later abortion, she was emotionally unavailable. Daniel grew up in a landscape of unspoken tension, carrying the weight of his father's absence and the family's silent grief entirely on his own.

The First Constellation: Breaking the Cycle of Ancestral Aggression

The initial work focused on the shame of the abuse and the hidden systemic link between the cousin's actions and the family's unmourned history.

While the abuse felt like an isolated event, the constellation revealed that the violence did not start with the cousin; it was a ghost from the maternal line that began generations earlier with Daniel's Great Grandfather.

The Great Grandfather's Burden

The trauma originated with Daniel's Maternal Great Grandfather—a soldier and prisoner of war who suffered unspeakable violence leading to a mental breakdown. Because the family distanced itself from his "madness" and aggression, the burden became an unacknowledged energy that sought expression in later generations.

In systemic constellations, we observe that what is excluded by one generation is often "taken up" or "acted out" by a later one. This unintegrated violence first manifested as disruptive behavior in Daniel's Maternal Uncle. Rather than being met with healing, the Uncle was also sent away and excluded. This second exclusion intensified the pressure of the hidden trauma until it settled upon the Uncle's son—Daniel's cousin. The cousin became the unconscious carrier of this inherited aggression, manifesting the family's greatest unacknowledged burden through the act of abuse against Daniel.

Healing Movements: Separating Shame from Victimhood

The core of Daniel's healing lay in disentangling his identity from the trauma he endured. For years, Daniel had carried the abuse as a personal "stain." In the constellation, we worked to return that shame to its source.

By seeing the Cousin not as a lone predator, but as the final "carrier" of a century-old lineage of violence, Daniel could stop asking *"What is wrong with me?"* and start seeing *"What happened to us?"* I guided Daniel through the following movements:

1. **Acknowledging the Ancestor**: Daniel faced the representative of the Great Grandfather:

   "Great grandfather, I see your pain. You also have a place in this family."

2. **Externalizing the Burden**: Daniel then faced the Cousin:

   "I see why you are the way you are, but I release this burden — it's not mine to carry."

Daniel felt a wave of calmness replace his old inner tension, describing it as a feeling of distance from the abuse. That final healing sentence was the big "Aha!" moment. It completely flipped the script: the abuse wasn't Daniel's personal failure or something he deserved; it was just a symptom of that massive, unhealed trauma inherited through the family line. We acknowledged the Cousin's entanglement with that inherited aggression, but made sure Daniel knew he wasn't responsible for the historical baggage. By returning that heavy burden to the system where it belonged, Daniel finally stepped out of the shame and isolation, reclaiming his own identity.

Reclaiming Life and Reintegrating His Family

With the systemic burden released, it was crucial to bring this new, whole self into connection with his mother. Having separated himself from the inherited shame, the connection could now be clean.

I guided Daniel to face his Mother and say: **"Look at me, Mom. This wasn't my fault!"**

Daniel felt a softening in his throat and a clear sense of being witnessed for the first time. I then guided him to address the future, honoring her difficult choice while asserting his right to be whole:

> **"I love you, Mom, even if I choose to reconnect with them [the father's side and maternal family]."**

Daniel let out a long breath, feeling a deep settling in his belly. The statement honors his mother's protective choice while ending the "loyalty conflict" that had kept him fragmented. His mother reached out and embraced him without conditions. For the first time, Daniel felt safe in her arms—not just as her son, but as a child belonging to both parents.

The Second Constellation: Connecting With Parents & The Missing Sibling

While the first session cleared the shame of the abuse and restored the lineage, a lingering sense of loneliness remained. A second, separate constellation was necessary to address the specific "coldness" and isolation Daniel felt from his parents.

The Constellation Set-Up

We set up representatives for Daniel, his mother, his father, the aborted child, and his paternal grandfather.

The paternal grandfather was also a war veteran with a deep history of trauma that cast a shadow over his entire family. In the field, the Father stood completely frozen, his back turned to Daniel and his eyes fixed on the Paternal Grandfather. He was emotionally locked in the past, unable to turn around and see his living children.

Across the room, the Mother was similarly distracted. She was looking down at the representative for the aborted child who lay on the floor. Daniel was also looking at the aborted child, unconsciously pulled toward the sibling who had no place.

Honoring the Father's Bond

The father's emotional distance wasn't a lack of love, but an unconscious preoccupation with his own father's war trauma. In systemic work, we see that children often feel rejected when a parent is "looking at the dead." Daniel had spent his life trying to get his father's attention, not realizing his father was trapped in a different time.

I asked Daniel to say to his father: **"I respect your love for your father."**

As he spoke, Daniel's body relaxed. He began to see his father as a whole person for the first time—not as a source of rejection, but as a man bound by his own loyalties. By acknowledging the father's primary bond with his own lineage, Daniel could finally stop trying to "fix" his father and be the "small one" again. As the truth was acknowledged, the father's representative finally exhaled and turned to look at Daniel with warmth for the first time.

Honoring the Aborted Child and Reclaiming the Mother

In Family Constellations, the fundamental rule is that everyone has an equal right to belong. The isolation Daniel felt was actually the "energy" of the excluded sibling. When a child is lost and not mourned, the living children often feel a subconscious pull toward the "void" left behind, as if they are trying to keep the sibling company in the "unseen."

I asked Daniel to face the representative for the aborted child on the floor and say:

"I see you. You are my sibling, and you have a place in our family."

As he spoke, Daniel felt a deep wave of recognition for the sibling he had been missing his whole life. In giving this child a place, Daniel restored the natural Order of Birth; he no longer had to unconsciously occupy that "lost" space. This move from secret shame to the truth allowed him to finally claim his rightful position in the family with a renewed sense of self-respect.

To complete the healing and restore the connection with his mother, I asked Daniel to face her directly. She was still standing with her head bowed, her gaze locked on the representative of the aborted child in a state of frozen grief. I asked him to say:

"I respect your love for your child."

As he spoke, by agreeing to her grief instead of competing for her attention, the barrier between them dissolved. Daniel felt a surge of relief; he no longer had to stand in the space of the missing sibling just to be near her. His mother's representative slowly raised her head and finally met his eyes, her heart freed from the secret "hold" of the lost child.

Conclusion: A Restored Sense of Belonging

Through these two layers of work, Daniel moved from a place of secret shame and crushing isolation to a place of truth. He stopped being the carrier of ancestral aggression and the substitute for lost siblings. He walked into his life not as a caretaker or a victim, but as a man who is the sum of all his parts, finally grounded in his own history.

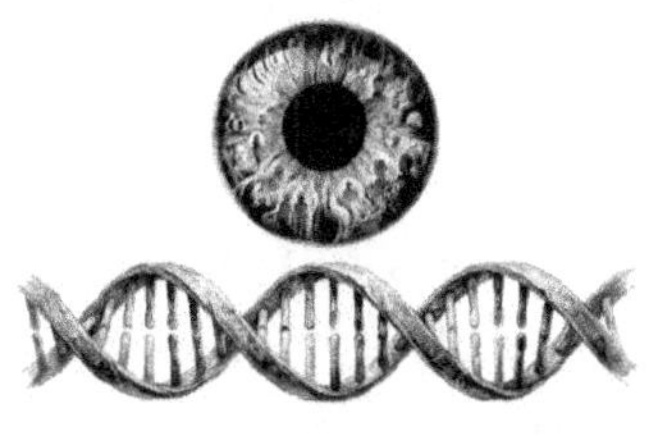

Chapter 20

Isolation: Denise Wants To Belong

Denise entered the therapeutic space burdened by a profound sense of emotional isolation and exclusion. She described a persistent inability to find her "rightful place" within her family, a struggle underpinned by the heavy, often invisible weight of generational trauma. Her family history reveals a complex web of abandonment, violence, and systemic entanglements that left her disconnected from her own strength.

The Fragile Maternal Bond and Generational Absence

Denise's earliest years were marked by a significant rupture; her mother immigrated to Europe, leaving Denise behind until she was four years old. During this formative period, Denise was moved between various caregivers, including her maternal aunt, cousin, and paternal grandmother—the singular pillar of her early life. However, this period of safety ended in trauma when her mother returned and took her to Europe, abruptly severing the only secure attachment she had known.

To compound this immense pain, Denise only discovered years later that her grandmother had passed away. Her absent father had kept this information from her, and she only learned of the death when she finally reconnected with him. Finding out that she had been denied the chance to mourn the woman who raised her was a painful blow—a discovery that solidified her feeling of being excluded from her family's history and belonging.

The relationship with her mother was further complicated by the mother's own history of growing up in an environment of extreme violence. This shaped a maternal bond that was toxic, volatile, and emotionally distant. Denise found herself trapped in a "parentified" role, forced to navigate a fluctuating dynamic where she was at times the daughter, at times a sister, at times an adversary, and frequently the "mother" to her own parent.

The Shadow of Exclusion: The Unborn

The systemic field was also heavily influenced by a history of profound loss regarding the unborn. Denise's mother was a survivor of multiple abortions (the grandmother had several abortions, with Denise's mother being one of the few who survived to be born). Furthermore, Denise's mother had undergone an abortion herself. These layers of systemic exclusion created a field of "missing" siblings and children that Denise was unconsciously carrying.

Personal Trauma and the Cycle of Violence

Denise's personal history was marred by the presence of her stepfather, a man with a criminal history who once attempted to strangle her. This event led to a violent altercation and resulted in two hospitalizations for her mother. In systemic terms, the mother's choice of a violent partner likely reflected an unconscious compulsion to repeat the chaotic dynamics of her own family of origin—a tragic search for the "familiar" through destructive relational patterns.

Compounding this sense of disconnection was Denise's own abortion at age twenty. At the time of our work, the full emotional impact of this loss had not yet been realized, sitting as a silent, unintegrated layer of grief within her already fractured sense of self.

Family Rejection

Denise's father remained emotionally distant, eventually remarrying and fathering a son. Denise remained unaware of her father's new life until she was ten years old. Any hope of reconciliation was blocked by his new wife, who denied Denise contact and intensified her existing feelings of rejection.

The Constellation Set-Up

To begin the healing process, I first set up a constellation representing Denise, her mother, her father, and the maternal grandmother (GM-m). I also asked for a representative for the aborted sibling (Denise's sibling) to lay on the floor.

Parental Distance and Entanglements:

The physical positioning of the representatives revealed a profound systemic fracture. While the representatives for the mother and father remained distant, the mother stood in close, almost clinging proximity to the representative for Denise. Meanwhile, Denise's maternal grandmother (GM-m) stood with her eyes fixated on the floor—a gaze the mother seemed instinctively drawn to follow. This shared focus suggested they were both energetically tethered to the grandmother's lost children.

Because the grandmother's emotional capacity was consumed by her own trauma—the grief of a violent family history and the weight of multiple abortions—she remained unavailable to her daughter. This created a "systemic void." In an unconscious attempt to fill this emptiness, Denise's mother sought fulfillment through her own child, casting Denise in the role of a surrogate mother.

This dynamic is a classic systemic mechanism: a parent who was emotionally starved in childhood turns to their offspring to settle their unmet needs. By reversing the *Hierarchy of Giving and Receiving,* the mother effectively demanded the care and emotional validation she was owed by the previous generation, forcing Denise to provide the nurturing she should have been receiving.

Denise's Heart: The Longing for a Father's Presence

The father's representative stood at a quiet distance, his gaze turned away from both Denise and her mother. It wasn't necessarily a gesture of unkindness, but rather a reflection of a heart that was elsewhere—emotionally unavailable and unable to meet the family's needs in that moment.

Meanwhile, the representative for Denise watched him with a tender, heavy sadness. Every part of her seemed to be reaching out, her eyes fixed on the distant father she so deeply loves and misses. This "sad staring" was actually a profound expression of her daughterly devotion—a desperate, soulful hope that if she only looked long enough, he might turn around and see her. It is a poignant reminder of how much of Denise's inner light is currently focused on trying to bridge the gap between her and her father, leaving her with a beautiful but empty heart.

Healing Movements

Reclaiming Her Own Place

The most delicate thread we initially followed was Denise's quiet, unconscious pull toward her excluded sibling. In the invisible map of the family, she had been standing in a space that wasn't hers, drawn by a deep, sisterly loyalty to someone who had been forgotten.

To begin the healing, Denise stepped into the circle herself, replacing her representative to feel the shift in her own body. I invited her to lie down beside the representative of the aborted child—not to stay there, but to finally acknowledge them. For a long while, we simply waited. It was a sacred, silent moment of recognition where Denise could finally say, with her presence,

"I see you. You belong."

As this connection settled into her heart, a visible weight began to lift. Denise was able to let go of the sibling's hand, not out of rejection, but out of a peaceful realization that she didn't need to carry their fate anymore. She stood up—noticeably taller, straighter, and with a new sense of belonging. She was no longer a shadow; she was becoming herself.

To anchor this new strength, Denise looked into her mother's eyes and spoke her true place into existence:

"I am the second of three children." "I am the second daughter."

As she claimed these words, the cloudiness in her gaze cleared. It was as if she were seeing her mother—and being seen by her—for the very first time as she truly is. This reconnection to her mother, rooted in her own right to exist, served as the beautiful foundation we needed before moving deeper into the family story.

Reclaiming Her Place: The Daughter's Return

As Denise's confidence began to bloom, the deeper architecture of the family needed to be addressed. We moved to resolve a "Hierarchy Imbalance"—a heavy, invisible role Denise had taken on to fill the void left by her grandmother's absence in her mother's life. For years, Denise had been her mother's emotional anchor, a "mother to her own mother," a role that is both exhausting and out of alignment with the flow of love.

To restore the natural order, I invited Denise to look at her mother and gently but firmly return the parental weight she had been carrying:

"Mom, you are the Big One, and I am the Little One."
"You are the mother, and I am the daughter."

As these words filled the room, the shift was immediate. The mother's representative took a small, instinctive step back, finally standing on her own feet. Denise let out a long, shuddering sigh of relief—the kind of breath that only comes when a lifelong burden is finally set down.

In that moment, Denise's energy changed. She seemed to "shrink" back into her rightful size as a child, finding the safety and humility of being smaller than her parent. This was not a loss of power, but a gain of freedom. By no longer having to be her mother's protector, she was finally free to turn her gaze elsewhere. The unconscious chains of loyalty were broken, clearing the path for her to finally reach out toward her father.

Honoring the Father: From Longing to Liberation

With the umbilical entanglement to her mother resolved, Denise was finally standing in her own space. For the first time, she could feel her authentic longing for her father without the cold shadow of guilt or the fear of betraying her mother. She was no longer a shield for her mother; she was a daughter looking for her source.

I asked her to turn and face her father directly. The air in the room shifted as she spoke the words she had silenced for decades:

"Dad, I wanted you to look at me. I've waited all my life for your love."

As tears traced paths down her cheeks, the "proper" Denise - the one who had tried to be okay with his absence - fell away. In her place stood a woman speaking a raw, somatic truth. Her father's representative met her gaze and nodded slowly, a solemn acknowledgment of the years of distance and the depth of her ache. This recognition was the medicine she had been seeking.

However, the final step of her journey required a transition from the "wounded child" to the "sovereign adult." To truly move forward, Denise needed to release the unconscious competition she felt with his new life. She had to honor the reality of his current world to stop being a ghost in it.

I guided her to say:

"I respect your love for your son and your new wife."

As she uttered these words, a profound stillness settled over her. This wasn't a concession; it was a release of the "unconscious demands" that had kept her stuck in a cycle of seeking approval. Her father's representative visibly relaxed, his shoulders dropping as the pressure of her expectations lifted.

In recognizing her father's right to his own life, Denise finally claimed the right to hers. She was no longer the rejected child waiting by the door; she was a free adult, standing on her own ground, ready to walk into a future defined by her own choices rather than her family's history.

Conclusion: The Importance of Sequence in Constellation Work

In the architecture of a constellation, the sequence of healing movements is not arbitrary; it is a clinical and systemic necessity. Drawing from my background in **Gestalt therapy,** I have found that a client often lacks the internal support or "ground" to fully process personal trauma - such as Denise's own abortion or the violence she endured from her stepfather - until the foundational entanglements with their family of origin are untangled.

In Denise's case, we prioritized a specific order of operations:

1. **Anchoring the Self:** Addressing the excluded sibling first to secure Denise's true place in the family hierarchy.
2. **Restoring the Mother-Daughter Bond:** Clearing the "parentification" and historical trauma to allow Denise to return to the role of the child.
3. **Honoring the Father's Reality:** Relinquishing the competition for his attention by acknowledging his new family structure.

While the energy of Denise's personal loss (her abortion) was palpably present, the systemic disturbances involving her parents held precedence. Trying to process an individual loss while still carrying the weight of a parent's history is like trying to heal a wound while the body is in a state of chronic exhaustion.

By resolving these primary entanglements first, we enabled Denise to step into her full adult strength. This sequence ensures that her personal grief can be addressed in a subsequent session from a position of "sovereignty." She will no longer be processing her loss as an entangled child, but as a grounded adult who has finally reclaimed her place in the world.

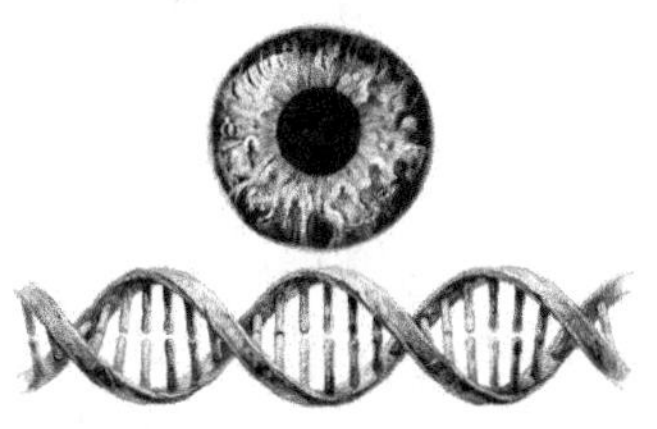

Chapter 21

Abortions & Self Esteem: Angelica's Right to Be a Mother

Angelica arrived at the retreat carrying the heavy weight of years spent in the shadows of low self-esteem and a quiet, persistent sense of self-betrayal. Behind her tendency to please others and her profound sense of guilt lay a heart that felt it had lost its right to belong, especially to the world of mothers.

The Weight of the Past: A Story of Two Hearts

As we gently explored her family history, it became clear that her deepest pain was held in the memory of two lost pregnancies, each a different kind of heartbreak:

1. **The First Loss (The Stolen Choice):** At just fifteen, Angelica was forced by her mother to have an abortion. This wasn't just a medical event; it was a foundational violation of her young spirit. It set a painful pattern in her life where her own voice was silenced by the wills of others, teaching her early on that her heart's desires were not her own to keep.

2. **The Second Loss (The Burden of Silence):** Years later, when she found herself pregnant again, Angelica truly wished to keep the child. However, the old echoes of the past returned, and she yielded to the pressure of those around her. This second loss deepened the original wound, leaving her with a debilitating shame and the belief that her needs simply did not matter.

The systemic core of her suffering was a double exclusion: the two children had no place in the family's memory, and Angelica, caught in unresolved grief, had excluded herself from the beautiful, life-giving flow of motherhood.

The Constellation: A Path Toward Peace

We began the constellation with a representative for Angelica and a representative to hold the space for her two children. Our goal was to create a bridge of love:

- To honor the two children and bring them back into the warmth of the family heart.
- To gently lift the burden of guilt from Angelica's shoulders, allowing her to stand tall in her own life once again.

The Intervention: A Journey of Reconciliation

1. **A Heart-to-Heart Acknowledgment** The first healing movement began when Angelica stepped into the circle to look into the eyes of the representative of her children. The atmosphere in the room softened as she faced the pain she had carried alone for so long. I invited her to speak from the depth of her soul:

"Dear Children, I am sorry."

The moment those words were whispered, the energy shifted from a painful memory to a living reconciliation. Angelica moved to the floor, curling into a fetal position beside the representative of her children. They held one another and cried together—a sacred release of shared grief and a long-awaited bridge of forgiveness. As the representative for the children felt a sense of lightness and peace, the heavy chains of shame began to fall away from Angelica.

2. **Welcomed Back into the Circle of Mothers** To complete her journey, we moved to heal her connection to the collective strength of women. I asked the mothers in the group to come forward. They gathered around Angelica, resting their hands on her shoulders and back, creating a physical "nest" of support. In that moment, Angelica was no longer alone; she was being held by the collective life force of womanhood.

In the middle of this circle of support, I spoke the final, transformative truth:

"You have a right to be a mother."

As she took in these words, a deep validation washed over her. The lifelong belief that she had forfeited her place in the world of mothers was replaced by a profound sense of belonging. The sentence served as a gentle invitation, calling her home to the natural flow of life and the unconditional right to love and be a mother.

A few months after our retreat, Angelica wrote something very touching to me:

"A lot has changed for the better – I've been able to stay in recovery and remain sober, stay committed to daily meditation and meetings,

return to my music, and leave a very dangerous, toxic relationship. Breaking that narcissistic abuse cycle allowed me to regain my independence and start making decisions aligned with my true moral compass."

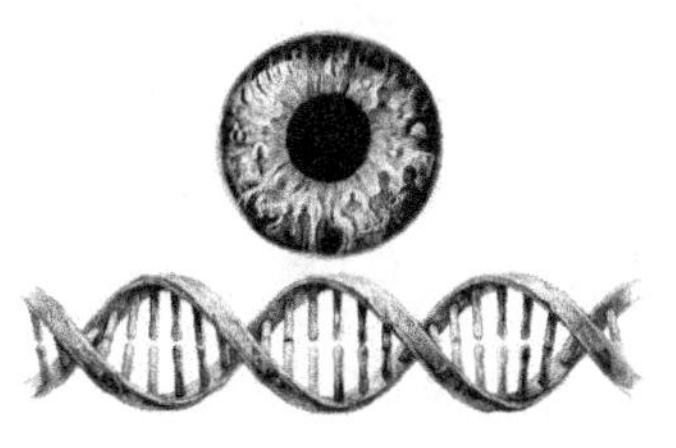

Chapter 22

Relationships & Men: Rumi's Brother & Father

A year later, Rumi returned to another retreat. The initial relief had settled and she no longer had pain between her shoulders. However, this time, a deeper, more heavy-set layer was ready to emerge from the shadows. Rumi spoke of a lifelong prohibition: she was not allowed to show emotions as a child. She carried a profound sense of responsibility for the emotional well-being of the men in her life, a burden that seemed to echo through her history of two abortions and a subsequent miscarriage with her husband.

The Field of the Displaced Aunt

As I guided Rumi into the field, we began with her mother and grandmother. Rumi's mother was a dominant, forceful woman—the eldest of five. We discovered a tragic break in the family soul: one of the mother's sisters had been given away to an uncle who had no children.

In systemic theory, the "Order of Precedence" demands that everyone has an equal right to belong. When a child is "given away," even to a relative, the family soul views it as an exclusion. Rumi's grandmother had lived in a state of perpetual, frozen grief for this "missing" daughter, leaving her emotionally unavailable to the children who remained. Rumi's mother, in turn, had stepped up as the eldest to carry the responsibility for her younger siblings, effectively losing her own childhood.

In the constellation, Rumi stood frozen. She felt respect for her mother, but no love. Her heart, however, was wide open for her grandmother and the aunt who was given away. This is a classic identification; Rumi was looking past her mother toward the "excluded" ones, trying to give them the love they never received.

Returning the Fate

I asked Rumi to look at her grandmother and then at her aunt. I guided her to speak the words that began to untangle these energetic threads:

"I am not Martelie [the child given away]. I am Rumi."

And then to the representative for her aunt who was given away:

"I am not you. I am Rumi."

Rumi took in a deep breath as her misplaced identification began to dissolve. Rumi was no longer the placeholder for a lost child; she was simply herself. Then, I directed her to the most difficult movement: acknowledging her mother. Rumi's mother was standing there, longing for her own mother's love, weeping for what she never received. We see here the "interrupted reaching out" passed down through generations.

I guided Rumi to say to her mother:

"I respect your longing for your mother."

The moment the words left her lips, Rumi's body softened. Years of unmet expectations and the heavy static of "what should have been" seemed to evaporate, allowing her to see her mother with a newfound, quiet respect. I then invited Rumi to lie at her mother's feet—the ultimate gesture of humility and "Smallness" in systemic work. By placing herself physically below her mother, Rumi was finally surrendering the exhausting "Big" role she had been forced to play since childhood.

As she lay there, the tension in her heart began to ease. A profound sense of freedom washed over her. She was no longer the guardian of the family burden; she was just the child.

The Mirror of the Brother & The Masculine

The final movement addressed Rumi's tendency to "carry" the men in her life. After her father's death when she was eighteen, Rumi had stepped into a pseudo-masculine role as the family's emotional anchor, feeling particularly responsible for her then eleven-year-old brother.

To reorder this, I placed a representative for her brother in the center of the room. Behind him, I carefully positioned representatives for their parents and grandparents. This was done so that Rumi could get a visual and somatic sense of the support existing behind him.

As Rumi watched this, a wave of relief surged through her. Her body physically shook as she released the exhausting and misplaced responsibility she had carried for decades. The image was undeniable: he had his own parents and ancestors to hold him; Rumi was finally relieved of the need to be his surrogate mother.

I then applied this same systemic lens to her relationship with the masculine in general. I brought in a representative for a partner—a symbol of the man she might one day fully let in—and stood a line of his own ancestors behind him. It was a powerful sight: a man who didn't need her to be his foundation because he was already standing on the shoulders of giants.

This visual shift allowed Rumi to finally breathe; she saw that a man carries his own history, his own weight, and his own strength. She didn't have to provide the floor for him to stand on. Looking into the eyes of this representative, I guided her to speak the words that shattered the old pattern:

"You are not my brother"

"Wooooowwwwww!!" Rumi exclaimed… A light suddenly broke across her face. She glowed with a mischievous look and a wide, flirty smile. *"Gosh, I wish I was thirty years younger!"*

We all burst into deep laughter with her. Rumi, this very special seventy five year old woman on a deep spiritual path, still had the spark to move the whole room.

A Few Days After The Retreat…

As the constellation closed, Rumi left the circle feeling unburdened and soft, moving with a feminine ease she hadn't known since she was a young girl. The shift was immediate and magnetic; a few days after the retreat, Rumi wrote to me, delighted that new men were suddenly flirting with her and stopping to offer her rides. It was as if the world finally recognized she was no longer a guardian to be leaned upon, but a woman ready to be seen in her own right.

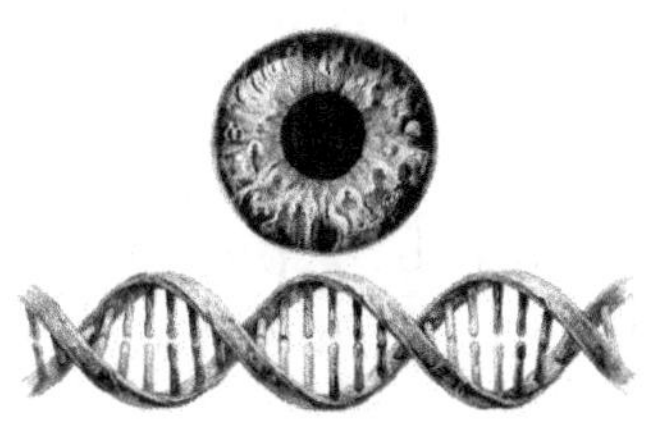

Chapter 23

Ashamed of My Mother: Maria Receives The Gift of Life

Maria came to me to explore her history, having grown up in a profoundly turbulent household. Her mother battled severe psychiatric issues, swinging between extreme excitement and deep depression. These unpredictable mood swings created a chaotic life for Maria, leaving her feeling embarrassed, isolated, and emotionally dependent on her mother's erratic behavior.

A key event defining Maria's isolation occurred at age 15 when her mother interrupted a study session with an emotional breakdown. The shame from this led Maria to never invite friends home again, deepening her loneliness. Although Maria established a stable adult life as a nurse, wife, and mother of a 13-year-old daughter, she carried lingering shame, emotional distance from her mother, and unresolved childhood pain.

The Constellation Breakthrough and Lasting Peace

Our session aimed to untangle the adult Maria from the child's inherited emotional burden. The goal was to move beyond the painful entanglement and confront the foundational truth of their systemic relationship.

I asked her to bow toward the representative of her mother and speak the simple, profound sentence of acceptance:

"You gave me life, thank you."

As the words settled, Maria paused, letting the statement permeate her body. She then acknowledged that beneath the decades of pain and shame lay an undeniable, essential love. The pivotal systemic movement was the profound acceptance of the biological gift.

As Maria truly surrendered to the *primal bond between mother and daughter, the source of her very being,* the biological truth began to integrate, gradually overpowering the structure of the childhood shame. This quiet revolution brought a deep, significant softening to her inner conflict. The decades of shame dissolved, allowing for a cleaner, more authentic flow of connection to the woman *who gave her life.*

Impact On Future Generations

This peace doesn't just heal her past, it transforms her present. Maria now stands anchored in a place of deep love and respect for her mother, recognizing the fundamental connection between them. No longer tethered to the trauma's orbit, she is liberated to be fully present as a mother to her daughter. Her 13-year-old daughter will feel the systemic shift, benefiting from a mother who is whole and untangled from the past.

This is the enduring power of healing generational trauma: *It frees up our children and future generations from unconscious inherited burdens.*

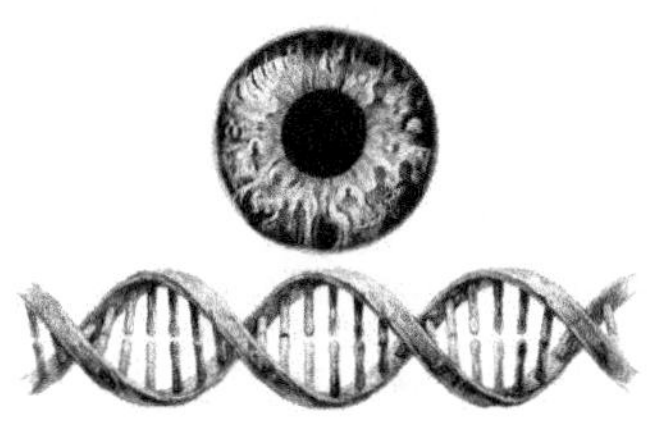

Chapter 24

Conclusion & Your Next Steps

Thank you for witnessing these profound stories of courage and transformation. As you went through these stories, you may have felt a resonance within your own heart. Perhaps you recognized a burden you've been carrying that was never yours to bear, or an imbalance that no longer serves you.

As you approach these final pages of your journey, I invite you to look at your own life through the systemic lens of these stories. Ask yourself:

- *Who is missing from my heart?*
- *Whose burden am I carrying out of a mistaken sense of loyalty?*
- *What truth am I finally ready to see?*

Healing is not about changing your history, but about changing your relationship to it. Once you understand the laws of the systemic field, you can no longer be lost. You know that you now belong. And you know that even the most painful history can be transformed into the soil from which a new, vibrant life can grow.

A Heartfelt Invitation to Heal

While these pages have planted the seeds of insight, *your most vibrant growth and deep healing happens when we step into the "Field" together.* Whether you are seeking personal peace or a professional calling, I would be honored to walk beside you:

Gatherings, Retreats, and Training: There is a special magic in meeting in person. My retreats and professional trainings, held in beautiful parts of the world, offer safe spaces where we move from understanding into experience. Whether you are looking to find your own relief through Family Constellations and Trauma Healing, or wish to master this art to heal others, you will find a supportive community here that integrates trauma-informed care with a heart-centered approach.

Private Events: If you have a specific group, community, or organization that would benefit from this work, I facilitate private retreats or custom training sessions. These private events are a powerful way to heal the collective energy of your community. For professional groups, these trainings are also a vital resource for healers to improve your healing abilities, establish healthier professional boundaries, build emotional resilience, and improve self care.

Online Courses To Heal Your Mind & Body: To bridge the gap between theory and practice, my online courses offer a private, contemplative space to apply these principles to your own life. By integrating *family constellations, naturopathic medicine, homeopathy and trauma healing*, these programs facilitate a profound journey for both your mind and your body. Through powerful exercises, you will learn to let go of trauma and the systemic roots of physical or emotional symptoms. You will also deepen your understanding of inherited trauma and holistic medicine at your own pace, honoring the intricate connection between your health, your emotions, and your ancestry.

Private Sessions: Personal sessions are a great way to heal both your body and your mind more completely with a combination of naturopathic medicine, family constellations and trauma healing. Sessions can be online or in person where I travel to.

To join an upcoming retreat, discuss organizing a private event, or begin your journey in personal transformation with my courses and private sessions, please visit: **www.drameet.com**

With Love and Gratitude,

Ameet

A portion of the proceeds from my books support orphans and children living with disabilities and HIV, while also funding environmental tree-planting initiatives. To support these projects, please consider gifting a copy to your network, requesting your libraries and bookstores to carry this title, and leaving a helpful review online. Thank you.

www.ingramcontent.com/pod-product-compliance
Lightning Source LLC
Chambersburg PA
CBHW071334150726
47997CB00002B/713